Cassandra's Daughters

N.L. Terteling Library

Swisher Memorial Collection

Recent Titles in Contributions in Women's Studies

Cassandra's Daughters

The Women in Hemingway

Roger Whitlow

CONTRIBUTIONS IN WOMEN'S
STUDIES, NUMBER 51

GREENWOOD PRESS
WESTPORT, CONNECTICUT
LONDON, ENGLAND

Library of Congress Cataloging in Publication Data

Whitlow, Roger.
  Cassandra's daughters.

  (Contributions in women's studies, ISSN 0147-104X ;
no. 51)
  Bibliography: p.
  Includes index.
  1. Hemingway, Ernest, 1899–1961—Characters—Women.
2. Women in literature. I. Title. II. Series.
PS3515.E37Z948   1984   813'.52   84-521
ISBN 0-313-24488-X (lib. bdg.)

$95

**OCLC
10348436**

Library of Congress Catalog Card Number: 84-521
ISBN: 0-313-24488-X
ISSN: 0147-104X

First published in 1984

Greenwood Press
A division of Congressional Information Service, Inc.
88 Post Road West
Westport, Connecticut 06881

Printed in the United States of America

10 9 8 7 6 5 4 3 2 1

For MARY AGNES HERMES

Contents

Preface

One can hardly take on a project like the present one without a sense of trepidation, knowing, as we all do, Hemingway's feelings of condescension and contempt for literary critics. For Hemingway, literary critics were mostly parasites, "thesis-hunters," or simply writers who "couldn't cut it" any other way. And to be part of a profession that was looked upon with contempt by Hemingway is no small matter; putting aside the extreme critical claims—like Dwight Macdonald's charge that Hemingway was not even very intelligent,[1] and John O'Hara's counterclaim that Hemingway was the greatest writer since Shakespeare[2]—Hemingway's reputation is assured as one of the three or four most gifted American writers of this century. Indeed, more than a fine writer, Hemingway reached a celebrity status which, at the time of his death, made requisite letters of condolence from the White House, the Vatican, the Kremlin, and thousands of lesser places.[3]

Reasons beyond self-interest, however, compel me to undertake this task—to force a rethinking by Hemingway's reading public of several fundamental issues in the man's fiction, particularly the role of women in that fiction. It is not my purpose to demonstrate that some of Hemingway's "best friends" were women—who his best friends were I leave to such biographers as Carlos Baker, A. E. Hotchner, Mary Hemingway, Leicester Hemingway, and Gregory Hemingway. Nor is it my purpose to examine *why* Hemingway wrote what he did—I leave that to the individual and often contradictory special perspectives of Freudian critics like Philip Young, Jungians like Joseph DeFalco, existentialists like John Killinger, and feminists like Pamella Farley.

My chief purpose is to examine what the language of Hemingway's fiction says about his significant women characters and about the men with whom they are associated—to illustrate that the women characters have been consistently short-changed by critics. Forty years ago Edmund Wilson originated a negative "party-line" of criticism that has been adopted and perpetuated by two generations of Hemingway critics, including the most recent crop of Ph.D. candidates treating Hemingway's women in their dissertations. Much of the mind-set about Hemingway's women must be dispelled, not merely because the last decade has made it fashionable to rethink the "role of women," but because the language and logic of Hemingway's fiction itself demands it.

Among the many people who have helped me in one way or another during the three years of this project, I should like to offer special thanks to graduate assistants Devin Brown and George Brown for their research assistance, to Terri Newbill and Linda Highland for their excellent typing, to the Eastern Illinois University Faculty Research Council for a generous grant to support the project, and to James Quivey, Chairman of the English Department at Eastern, for providing helpful teaching-schedule arrangements, research and clerical assistance, and various other forms of support and encouragement.

Cassandra's Daughters

I

Hemingway, the Women,
and the Critics

THE CRITICS ON HEMINGWAY

The relationship between Ernest Hemingway and his critics was an oddly stormy one much of the time. Partly, no doubt, because of his salty impatience with those whose livelihoods depended upon interviewing and writing about such people as himself, Hemingway inspired in some critics a hostility similar to that which Richard Nixon would later inspire in newsmen. The impatience grew from a deep conviction that reviewers, interviewers and critics tended to ask inane questions about such things as his private relationships, his symbolism, or his "subconscious" motivations, to print misinterpretations of his answers, and to pursue, regardless of what he said, prejudgments about his work. There was, in fact, an unbecoming critical eagerness, at several stages in his career, to pronounce Hemingway dead, or at least badly crippled, as a writer.

Following the publication of *To Have and Have Not* in 1937, for example, Delmore Schwartz claimed that the novel was "a stupid and foolish book, a disgrace to a good writer, a book which should never have been printed." [1] At Hemingway's next critical low point, following the publication of *Across the River and into the Trees* in 1950, Maxwell Geismar would say: "It is not only Hemingway's worst novel; it is a synthesis of everything that is bad in his previous work and it throws a doubtful light on the future."[2] I hasten to add that these two novels are probably Hemingway's weakest—though each has considerable merit nonetheless. I maintain, however, that, as frequently happens to those who achieve distinction early in their careers, the critics were very exacting in their judgments of Hemingway's work; some took unfortunate delight in pointing out when he fell short of the expected mark.

On balance, however, the verdict has been quite favorable. The favorable pronouncements may fall somewhat short of John O'Hara's claim that Hemingway was the greatest writer since Shakespeare,[3] but they are powerful endorsements and they come from notable people. Joseph Warren Beach says that "contemporary American fiction opens with Ernest Hemingway";[4] Michael F. Moloney that Hemingway is "the most considerable figure in American fiction in the past quarter of a century";[5] Conrad Aiken that Hemingway "is in many respects the most exciting of contemporary American writers of fiction";[6] Arthur Koestler that Hemingway "[was] still the greatest living writer";[7] and Carlos Baker that "He was one of the foremost writers that America has produced, an epoch-making stylist with a highly original talent who spawned imitators by the score and dealt, almost single-handed, a permanent blow against the affected, the namby-pamby, the pretentious, and the false."[8]

All of the commentary has not been so favorable. A significant number of critics have called Hemingway's work—or, more often, his fictional world—"limited" in one way or another. Philip Young says that Hemingway is "a limited yet unmistakably major American writer."[9] Maxwell Geismar says that "Hemingway's fiction does seem more like an enchanted island than a complete world."[10] John Aldridge observed in 1951 that, while twenty years earlier Hemingway had been a "kind of twentieth-century Lord Byron" for a young generation, "the Hemingway time is dead now. It ended when the last echoes of the lost Twenties finally stopped reverberating in the early Forties, when the young men had to stop reminiscing about the first

Great War (which none of them could remember) in order to start thinking about the second Great War."[11]

Virginia Woolf found him skilled but "too self-consciously virile" and possessed of a talent that "had contracted instead of expanding,"[12] and Leon Edel insists that Hemingway "belongs to the second shelf of American fiction, not the first: he can safely be placed beside Sinclair Lewis rather than beside Hawthorne, Melville, or James."[13] But one of the fullest attacks has come from Dwight Macdonald, who is partly right when he asserts, along with many others, that Hemingway's significance "is almost entirely as a stylistic innovator"[14]—but he does not stop there. Macdonald uses a parody of that innovative style in his attack on Hemingway:

He was a big man with a bushy beard and everybody knew him. The tourists knew him and the bartenders knew him and the critics knew him too. He enjoyed being recognized by the tourists and he liked the bartenders but he never liked the critics very much. He thought they had his number. Some of them did. The hell with them. He smiled a lot and it should have been a good smile, he was so big and bearded and famous, but it was not a good smile. It was a smile that was uneasy around the edges as if he was not sure he deserved to be quite as famous as he was famous. . . .

He got more and more famous and the big picture magazines photographed him shooting a lion and catching a tuna and interviewing a Spanish Republican militiaman and fraternizing with bullfighters and helping liberate Paris and always smiling bushily and his stuff got worse and worse. Mr. Hemingway the writer was running out of gas but no one noticed it because Mr. Hemingway the celebrity was such good copy. . . .

He wrote a novel called *Across the River and into the Trees*. It was not a good novel. It was a bad novel. It was so bad that all the critics were against it. Even the ones who had liked everything else. The trouble with critics is that you can't depend on them in a tight place and this was a very tight place indeed. They scare easy because their brains are where their *cojones* should be and because they have never stopped a charging lion with a Mannlicher double-action .34 or done any of the other important things. The hell with them.[15]

Macdonald's most penetrating shot comes with his overall assessment of Hemingway's work: "There is little evidence of thought in Hemingway's writing and much evidence of the reverse. . . . For all the sureness of his instinct as a writer, he strikes one as not particularly intelligent." [16]

Many others have pronounced on Hemingway, of course. Both his work and his life have seemed to demand it—his work because literary products are generally commented upon, and his life because Hemingway made such prodigious efforts to entwine it in his work, and to elevate both to a celebrity level of visibility. Partly because many of the more carping critics could not forgive Hemingway because they were not he; partly because he did not write like Henry James, or even Theodore Dreiser; partly because of his manner of handling such issues as manhood, sexuality, violence, or simply life itself—for these and other reasons the critics have criticized.

HEMINGWAY ON THE CRITICS

But Hemingway struck back. Despite George Plimpton's disclaimer that Hemingway did not dislike critics all that much,[17] Hemingway did hold critics and academics generally in contempt as parasites, nitpickers, and individuals pursuing theses about his and other "important" people's work with reasonably little regard for what that work actually said. In an interview with Plimpton, Hemingway revealed the sarcasm that became increasingly evident in interviews as he grew older. He said, "The fact that I am interrupting serious work to answer these questions proves that I am so stupid that I should be penalized severely. I will be. Don't worry." [18]

Hemingway's attitude is understandable. He was a man of considerable, easily threatened, ego. He thought of himself as doing very important work—trying, as he put it to Charles Scribner, "to knock Mr. Shakespeare on his ass." [19] For a man, then, who placed himself in that league, who looked on the completion of a good book as the equivalent of making a major medical discovery or formulating diplomacy affecting a significant part of the world, the continual barrage of questions from graduate students and their professors must have seemed much like the nuisance that a swarm of gnats creates for a thorough-bred race horse.

Yet, while he resented the graduate students—who "call me up in the middle of the night to get something to hang on me so they can get a Ph.D."[20] (a parasitic image confirmed by Dwight Macdonald when he said that, immediately following Heming-way's suicide, "the graduate students smile thinly as they real-ize that a definitive study of the complete *oeuvre* of Ernest Hemingway is now possible")[21]—Hemingway reserved his strongest verbal (and occasionally physical) blows for those who had taught them their trade. He always resented academics for not really being a "part of life"—for not running the bulls, not hunting the big game, not participating in the process of war-time dying—indeed he typified far better than most men the "man in the arena" about whom Theodore Roosevelt spoke with such admiration (largely, of course, because Roosevelt felt that he was describing himself):

It is not the critic who counts; not the man who points out how the strong man stumbles, or where the doer of deeds could have done them better. The credit belongs to the man who is actually in the arena, whose face is marred by dust and sweat and blood; who strives valiantly; who errs, and comes short again and again, because there is no effort with-out error and shortcoming; but who does actually strive to do the deeds. . . .

In response to a question about writers talking about their work, Hemingway said: "The better the writers the less they will speak about what they have written themselves. Joyce was a very great writer and he would only explain what he was doing to jerks [read: interviewers/academics]. Other writers that he respected were supposed to be able to know what he was doing by reading it."[22] In response to a question about the influence on his work of Gertrude Stein, Ezra Pound, or Max Perkins, he said: "I'm sorry but I am no good at these post-mortems. There are coroners literary and nonliterary provided to deal with such matters."[23] In response to a question about his symbolism, he said: "I suppose there are symbols since critics keep finding them. If you do not mind I dislike talking about them and being questioned about them. It is hard enough to write books and stories without being asked to explain them as well. Also it deprives the explainers of work. If five or six more good explainers can keep going why should I interfere with them?"[24]

Hemingway's position on critics is clear enough: Unlike "real" writers, most of them seem not bright enough to understand what an author writes simply by reading the work itself; they must ask the author what he "means" in his work, then use their own extrapolations of the author's answer to explain the work to their readers or students. Even worse in Hemingway's mind were those critics who use a "real" writer's work merely as a vehicle for peddling their own ideas—the "thesis-hunters" who shape their interpretations of an author's work, as Hemingway put it, "to the procrustean bed of their isms and dialectics."[25]

Among the Freudians, Jungians, existentialists, "moralists," feminists, and others who measured Hemingway's work according to a predetermined thesis about life, for Hemingway two of the most notable offenders were Philip Young and Charles Fenton. Mary Hemingway describes her husband's reaction to their interpretations of his work:

As earlier he had been upset and disturbed by Philip Young's psychoanalytic hypothesis that his work had been influenced by his leg wounds in July 1918, he was now being bothered and bedeviled by an instructor or professor from Yale, Charles Fenton, who had chosen to write his doctoral dissertation about Ernest's early writing at Oak Park High School and on the Kansas City *Star*. Fenton had sent a piece he had done about the Kansas City work, its inaccuracies of reporting clearly visible to Ernest. In a two-page single-spaced letter dated June 22, Ernest tried to explain:

" . . . Did anyone in the old days have any right to work on a man's past and publish findings while the man was alive unless he was running for public office or was a criminal? . . . Don't you think there is some legal way, such as an injunction, that invasion of privacy can be restrained? If you do not, let me know why without getting sore. . . .

"I don't know whether you went to Oak Park or just wrote out there. But I do know that the impression you would get from it is quite false.

"It used to have a North Prairie and a South Prairie. The North Prairie ran from a block beyond your (our) house as far as the Des Plaines River which then had plenty of pickerel in it up to Wallace Evan's game farm where we used to poach. Where you see an apartment building now there was usually a big old house with a lawn. Where you see subdivisions and row after row of identical houses there used to be the gypsy camps in the fall with their wagons and horses. . . .

"The point I am trying to make by talking all around it is that when you come into something thirty-five years late, you do not get the true gen. You get Survivors' gen. You can get statistics and badly remembered memories and much slanted stuff. But it is a long way from the true gen and I do not see what makes it scholarship. . . .[26]

In a witty response to a question about Philip Young's Freudian interpretation of his wound—that Hemingway's mortar wound in Italy in 1918 so traumatized him that it substantially shaped his entire writing career—Hemingway said with mock seriousness: "The effects of wounds vary greatly. Simple wounds which do not break bone are of little account. They sometimes give confidence. Wounds which do extensive bone and nerve damage are not good for writers, nor anybody else."[27] In a more personal, off-the-point, attack on Edmund Wilson for what Hemingway regarded as an inaccurate assessment of A Farewell to Arms, Hemingway claimed that he had met "more people than Wilson had, but also that he knew a good deal more about the pleasures of sexual intercourse."[28]

Hemingway did not stop with verbal assaults on his critics. In addition to keeping in his mind a critical "enemies list,"[29] by the 1950's he began doing physical violence to those having the audacity to challenge the quality of his work or his motives. As Maxwell Geismar notes, "More recently his answer to adverse criticism has been an offer to take on the offending critic in a duel, a boxing match, or any other bout of physical prowess."[30]

One of the saddest examples of this response to criticism is recorded by Carlos Baker in his description of a violent encounter in Max Perkins' office between Hemingway and his long-time adversary Max Eastman:

His affability was quickly dissipated, however, on the afternoon of Wednesday, August 11th, when he strode into Max Perkins's office and found Max Eastman sitting there. His resentment against Eastman for the "Bull in the Afternoon" review had been rankling for upwards of four years. . . . The two men shook hands and exchanged minor pleasantries. Perkins, relieved, had just settled back in his chair when Ernest, grinning broadly, ripped open his own shirt to expose a chest which, as Perkins said, was "hairy enough for anybody." Eastman laughed and Ernest, still grinning, opened Eastman's shirt to reveal a chest "as bare as a bald man's head." The contrast led to further laughter, and Perkins was just preparing for a possible unveiling of his own when Ernest suddenly flushed with anger.

"What do you mean," he roared at Eastman, "accusing me of impotence?"

Eastman denied it. He was just going on to further explanations when he caught sight of his own volume, *Art and the Life of Action*, which happened to be lying on Perkins's desk. It contained a reprint of "Bull in the Afternoon" and he thrust it at Ernest, saying, "Here. Read what I *really* said." . . .

But Ernest, his face contorted with rising anger, smacked Eastman in the face with the open book. Eastman instantly rushed at him, and Perkins, fearing that Eastman might be badly hurt, ran over to grab Ernest's arm. Just as he came around the corner of the desk, the adversaries grappled and fell.[31]

THE CRITICS ON THE WOMEN

Violent responses notwithstanding, some critics continued to fault Hemingway, in no area more strongly than in his portrayal of women. Their major objection has been that the female characterizations are weak, that the women are "too thin," or "two-dimensional," or that, because they emphasize only single facets of human personality, they are actually caricatures. More recently, feminist criticism has ridiculed some of the more "passive" women as sexual pawns for Hemingway's heroes, or social foils in contrast with which the Hemingway males can appear more masculine.

Like journalistic, sociological, or historical trends, literary criticism often perpetuates "conventional-wisdom" notions about works and authors. Such has been the case with Hemingway's women; for more than forty years, it has been virtually a critical "given" that the women are "weak." In 1950 Theodore Bardacke said that little "has been said of [Hemingway's] heroines beyond an acknowledgement of an antagonism towards women."[32] This has remained true until quite recently. Even recent criticism on the women, though there is more of it, has continued the tendency to be categorical.

Overwhelmingly the most popular critical manner of categorizing Hemingway's women has been to dichotomize them. Philip Young generalizes that the women "are either vicious, destructive wives like Macomber's, or daydreams like Catherine, Maria, and Renata";[33] Arthur Waldhorn that "Hemingway's women either caress or castrate";[34] Jackson Benson that in Hemingway we find "the girl who frankly enjoys sex and who is genuinely able to give of herself" *and* "the 'all-around bitch,' the aggressive, unwomanly female";[35] John Killinger that "Hemingway divides his women into the good and the bad, according to the extent to which they complicate a man's life. Those who are simple, who participate in relationships with the heroes and yet leave the heroes as free as possible [like the Indian girls, Marie Morgan, Catherine, Maria, and Renata], receive sympathetic treatment; those who are demanding, who constrict the liberty of the heroes, who attempt to possess them [like Marjorie, Margot Macomber, and Dorothy Bridges], are the women whom men can live without."[36] More recently, from Pamella Farley and others, the familiar dichotomy has a feminist edge:

In no piece of fiction or drama written by Hemingway is there a relationship between a man and a woman which is not degrading, including the idyllic romance genre where the woman is a cardboard slave existing solely to increase the stature of the man. If she deviates from this function, if a woman is not submissive and flat (like Catherine in *Farewell to Arms* or Maria in *For Whom the Bell Tolls*), she is a bitch (like Brett in *The Sun Also Rises* or Margot in "The Short Happy Life of Francis Macomber"). For independent women are not proper foils for the male hero whose superiority requires subservience, particularly from women.[37]

There have been variations on this fairly simple dichotomy, notably Lionel Trilling's claim that Hemingway's "men are all dominance and knowledge, the women all essential innocence and responsive passion,"[38] and André Maurois' view that "to Hemingway, as to Kipling, woman is both an obstacle and a temptation."[39] Other variations expand the categories of Hemingway's women from the familiar two to three, as Sharon Dean does, or even to six, as Leon Linderoth does. Dean adds to the "passive dream girl" and "bitch" categories a group called "lost women," which includes Catherine Barkley (usually placed in the "passive" category), Brett Ashley (often categorized as a "bitch"), and "to a lesser degree Maria," each of whom "feels [the conflict between isolation and society] and though she is largely condemned to isolation, she defies the forces that mold her in order to perform some good for the man she loves."[40]

Leon Linderoth sets up the most elaborate construct, categorizing Hemingway's women into "six amorphous groups."[41] Linderoth, in properly denouncing the usual dichotomy of Hemingway heroines as too simplistic, proposes instead the following six categories: 1. "mindless Indian girls"—"who demand nothing of a man, for they give nothing but their bodies"; 2. "tumbril-bait"—girls like Liz Coates, Catherine Barkley, Marjorie, Jig, Maria, and Renata, who "are easily identified by their long hair and their sweetly feminine ways—and by the way the world hurts them, usually through their lovers"; 3. the "relatively 'virgin' "—women like Helen ("Cross Country Snow"), Helen ("Kilimanjaro"), and Dorothy Bridges, who "though they do not actively corrupt a man, nonetheless cramp his style. These girls could well develop into true bitches of the Macomber type"; 4. "bitches by circumstance only"—women like Brett Ashley and Margot Macomber, about whom Hemingway "usually provides some explanation for their behavior, an explanation that while it may not absolve them of blame at least gives some understanding of the forces that made them what they are"; 5. "pure bitches"—women like Mrs. Elliot, Mrs. Adams, and Helene (*To Have and Have Not*), who "seem to be total corrupters of the men with whom they associate"; 6. "earth mothers"—Marie Morgan and Pilar, who, "despite their amorality . . . are closely allied with the spontaneous and natural in life." Though Linderoth's multiple-category description is cumbersome, it is a considerable improvement over most of the fairly simplistic dichotomy arrangements.

The most extreme of the critical judgments on Hemingway's women comes from Leslie Fiedler. Fiedler sets up a dichotomy of his own, relating exclusively to sexual activity. "In his earlier fictions, Hemingway's descriptions of the sexual encounter are intentionally brutal, in his later ones unintentionally comic."[42] Related to this observation is Fiedler's flat statement, "There are, however, no *women* in his books."[43] This is an odd and exceptionally limited perception of what women "are," given the many different characteristics which women can possess, and which, in Hemingway, they do possess. It is a perception as limited as that of Donald Heiney and others who cannot allow the notion of a woman of substantial emotional and physical strength and therefore feel compelled to explain such women as Pilar as having "a certain masculine quality about them."[44]

It is primarily in response to the often simplistic interpretations of Hemingway's women, made by Edmund Wilson, Philip Young, Leslie Fiedler, and a host of other critics, that I write this book. I shall demonstrate that most of Hemingway's female characters have strengths that have been consistently overlooked by such critics, who have too often merely adopted a posture toward the women held by the male characters with whom the women are associated. Catherine Barkley and the Spanish Maria, for example, have been glibly typed as "passive sex kittens." In fact, the novels in which they appear make plain the serious struggle each is engaged in as she works her way back from the brink of insanity through a blend of sheer will and therapeutic love. Marie Morgan offers through her own love ethic a strikingly favorable contrast to her thug husband, Harry, on whom most of the critical attention has been focused, much of it lauding Harry's behavior. Renata, instead of the "mindless love creature" she is uniformly made out to be, is a very perceptive young woman who, through her homemade psychoanalysis, constructs a cathartic experience that allows the turbulent mind of the dying Cantwell a peaceful way out.

The women typed as "Hemingway's bitches" have also been badly treated. Neither Brett Ashley nor Helen in "The Snows of Kilimanjaro" is, in fact, a bitch at all. Brett, like Catherine and Maria, is on the brink of insanity, but unlike them, cannot sense the way to restoration, and, unlike Frederick Henry and Robert Jordan, Jake Barnes is himself a psychological cripple, a further liability, and can afford her no help. Helen is a devoted and deeply loving woman who has been treated shabbily by her weak and self–serving husband, whose strange notions about her somehow "corrupting" him have been eagerly embraced by most of the critics who have commented on the story. Even Margot Macomber, from the single most misread of all Hemingway's works, while cantankerous at times, is definitely *not*, as she has been almost unanimously charged for two generations, a murderess. She is a more honest individual than either of her judges, her husband and the guide Robert Wilson, whose twisted perceptions have shaped nearly all of the criticism on the story. Dorothy Bridges in *The Fifth Column*, admittedly spoiled and insensitive, nonetheless measures rather tall when compared with the man making most of the judgments about her, Philip Rawlings, a KGB-style secret agent and assassin.

Even the "minor" women have been misread—Liz Coates and Nick's Marjorie, for example—because their men and their critics have largely failed to see the "woman's side" of the trauma of early love and sexual experience. Mrs. Elliot and Mrs. Adams, called "pure bitches" by Leon Linderoth, are rarely measured alongside Mr. Elliot and Dr. Adams, two men who are no more admirable than their wives but who have escaped the constant censure accorded the women. Even the unseen Helen in "Cross Country Snow" is treated by Nick and the critics as one who has somehow conspired to cause her own pregnancy as an inconvenience for Nick, with little commentary on Nick's role in the matter or, indeed, the even greater inconvenience which the pregnancy causes Helen herself.

My purpose, then, is not to explore why Hemingway wrote what he did about women, nor what he was "feeling" about women at any given stage of his career, but to explore what his language actually says about his female characters and the way they deal with the circumstances of their lives. Hemingway was well-known for saying that his job was to "put down what I see and what I feel in the best and simplest way I can tell it."[45] In creating his women characters and the complicated milieu in which each has to operate, Hemingway may actually have "put down" more than he knew and more than many of his critics have found.

II

Cassandra's Daughters

CATHERINE BARKLEY

Since its original publication nearly fifty years ago, *A Farewell to Arms* has met with a generally favorable reception. Though some critics have judged it harshly—Dwight Macdonald claiming that a rereading of *Farewell* found the novel had "aged and shriveled from what I remembered,"[1] and B. E. Todd in his original review calling the book "an epic of weariness"[2]—most have been generous in their appraisal. Clifton Fadiman, for example, says that *Farewell* is "not merely a good book but a remarkably beautiful book";[3] Malcolm Cowley says that *Farewell* is "almost universally regarded as the best American novel of World War I";[4] W. M. Frohock calls it "that rarest of modern successes, a completely serious and successful love story";[5] Samuel Shaw pronounces it "one of the great love stories in American literature."[6]

Such favorable observations do not mean that *Farewell* goes down well with all critics for all reasons. Some have charged that the war story and the love story do not integrate as well as they might. Others have claimed that Frederick Henry maintains an odd distance from the events of the war. But unquestionably the severest criticism is reserved for Catherine Barkley, who is

described variously as shallow, weak, even silly. Arthur Waldhorn is gentlest with his observation that "Catherine is *almost*
realistic";[7] on the other hand, we find Otto Friedrich, Philip
Young, and Dwight Macdonald going vigorously for Hemingway's throat. Friedrich calls Catherine "one of Hemingway's most
unreal creations."[8] Young charges that Catherine is "idealized
past the fondest belief of most people"[9] and Macdonald claims
that Catherine is "not a person but an adolescent daydream."[10]

Catherine, I hasten to reply, is none of these things—not unreal, not idealized, and not to be written off as a daydream. She
is a very real woman clinging, at the opening of the novel, to
the last few shreds of sanity and hoping that Frederick Henry
can help her make the fabric of her mind whole again. Here is
the principal problem with most of the interpretations of Catherine's character: most critics have chosen to overlook her deeply
troubled psychological state and have judged her actions and
speeches against "normal" human behavior. Of course, in such
a context, Catherine seems unreal indeed, particularly in the
opening scenes with Frederick:

> "Oh, darling," she said. "You will be good to me, won't you?"
> What the hell, I thought. I stroked her hair and patted her shoulder.
> She was crying.
> "You will, won't you?" She looked up at me. "Because we're going
> to have a strange life."[11] [P. 27]

And:

> She looked at me, "And you do love me?"
> "Yes."
> "You did say you loved me, didn't you?"
> "Yes," I lied. "I love you." I had not said it before.
> "And you call me Catherine?"
> "Catherine." We walked on a way and were stopped under a tree.
> "Say, 'I've come back to Catherine in the night.' "
> "I've come back to Catherine in the night."
> "Oh, darling, you have come back, haven't you?"
> "Yes."

"I love you so and it's been awful. You won't go away?"
"No. I'll always come back."[P. 31]

Catherine's awareness of her psychological frailty is obvious
throughout the novel. Early in the relationship, Catherine says:
"Please let's not lie when we don't have to. I had a very fine
little show and I'm all right now" (p. 32). Later, while Frederick recuperates in Milan, Catherine says: "I haven't been happy
for a long time and when I met you perhaps I was nearly crazy.
Perhaps I was crazy" (p. 120). Just before Frederick returns to
the front, he says, "I thought you were a crazy girl," and Catherine replies, "I was a little crazy" (p. 160). Near the end of
the novel, just before Catherine's childbirth scene, she says, "I
just woke up thinking about how I was nearly crazy when I first
met you" (p. 311).

Catherine is part of a series of Hemingway characters who
border on insanity—Nick Adams, whose "Big-Two-Hearted-
River" experience is little more than self-therapy; Brett Ashley,
whose loss (like Catherine's) of a young lover to war creates her
empty and unfulfillable nymphomania, but who (unlike Catherine) cannot perceive the way to her own restoration; the Spanish
Maria, whose inhuman treatment by the Fascists has left her in
a state of near mental collapse and who is restored to balance
through the combined therapeutic measures of the mothering Pilar and the loving Robert Jordan; and Colonel Cantwell, whose
mind is entirely too disordered and whose attitude is too bitter
to prepare for death and who is skillfully led toward a sense of
self-peace by the young Renata.

More than any of these characters Catherine has the perception to understand what she must do to restore herself. Her most
pressing problems are three: she suffers severe guilt for refusing
sex to her young man before he went off to war; she suffers sorrow because of the young man's death; and she suffers fear of
her own death, the death of someone she loved having brought
her own mortality sharply to mind. Little can be done about
Catherine's fear of death, accentuated by her premonitions of
seeing herself "dead in the rain." Consciousness of one's own

mortality is quite a natural part of human thought and need not, of itself, be a cause for insanity. There are religious or philosophical constructs which mute the fear of death by promising another life or casting the individual as a part of the larger historical process in which all must die. Neither of these constructs works for Catherine.

By using Frederick as an unwitting therapist, however, Catherine can overcome her sense of guilt and loss and at the same time regain her sanity. The first problem, guilt for not having sex with her young man, she reveals to Frederick almost immediately upon their meeting: "I wanted to do something for him. You see I didn't care about the other thing and he could have had it all. He could have had anything he wanted if I would have known" (p. 19). Catherine seeks to overcome this guilt by her almost precipitous sexual arrangement with Frederick. Thus Catherine relieves her sense of responsibility to her dead young man, temporarily blurring the distinction between the young man and Frederick, and protects herself from further guilt should Frederick (whom she sees distinctly as himself much of the time) be killed. The sense of loss is first diminished when she blurs the identities of the two men, so that her young man still seems alive; later, as she comes to love Frederick for himself, the loss of the young man is almost completely forgotten.

But what of Frederick's role in the love relationship—and in the war? Most readers and critics agree that Frederick's reasons for being in Italy are thin indeed. Wyndham Lewis is quite right in saying that Frederick "has come over to Europe for the fun of the thing, as an alternative to baseball." [12] Hemingway himself would say, in 1942, of his own participation in the World War I Italian campaign: "I was an awful dope when I went to the last war. . . . I can remember just thinking that we were the home team and the Austrians were the visiting team." [13] Malcolm Cowley goes further. He claims that that perception extended to nearly a whole generation of Americans; the war, he says, "created in young men a thirst for abstract danger, not suffered for a cause but courted for itself." [14]

Frederick's own explanations for his presence in Italy bear out all three observations. When Catherine and Frederick first meet and she asks why he, an American, is involved, he says, "I don't know. . . . There isn't always an explanation for everything" (p. 18). And the next day, when Catherine asks once more why he joined the Italians, Frederick replies: "I was in Italy . . . and I spoke Italian" (p. 22). Still later, as Frederick muses over the possibility of being killed, he thinks: "Well, I knew I would not be killed. Not in this war. It did not have anything to do with me. It seemed no more dangerous to me myself than war in the movies" (p. 38).

From the start Hemingway shows some consciousness of the ironies and stupidities of the war milieu in which he places Frederick Henry. The first example of irony comes on the second page of the novel, when the narrator says: "At the start of the winter came the permanent rain and with the rain came the cholera. But it was checked and in the end only seven thousand died of it in the army" (p. 4). It is important to distinguish Hemingway's sense of irony "about life," however, from his less keen sense of irony about the war itself. It is through Frederick, in particular, that the ironies and stupidities about the war effort itself are revealed—his "treatment" by the cluster of incompetent doctors in the Milan hospital; his willing confession to Rinaldi that his valor at the front had been limited to the experience of being blown up while eating cheese; the later scramble of the Italian troops to abandon their weapons and return home; and, the crowning irony, the thoughtless murder by the Italian battle police of officers like Frederick Henry.

This brings me to one of the most significant points of this volume—the fact that many of Hemingway's heroes, certainly including Frederick Henry, have two courses of action available to them: the first, the pursuit of a mission that each has convinced himself is of value, usually even worth his own life; the second, the pursuit of those qualities usually embodied in the heroine with whom the hero is associated, the qualities of love, serving, devotion, and domesticity. J. F. Kobler is probably right when he says that Hemingway "has come to bury romantic love, not to praise it," but when he claims that Catherine "is in love only with love,''[15] he is as wrong as Leslie Fiedler when he says that all Catherine and Frederick wanted ''was innocent orgasm after orgasm.''[16]

If Hemingway has come to bury romantic love, he has offered a pathetic substitute in its place. He offers instead a Frederick Henry, who, though he has no real understanding of what he is doing on the Italian front, is nonetheless committed enough to return to the front following his recovery, committed enough to kill the runaway Italian sergeant for failing to follow the ''rules'' of wartime which Henry himself has already acknowledged are no longer valid. When Joseph Warren Beach says that in *Farewell* ''there is a positive reaction against something conceived as bad (the War) in favor of something conceived as good, the life together of a man and a woman who love each other,''[17] he overlooks the fact that Hemingway never condemns ''the War'' itself, but only the isolated stupidities of individuals connected with it. Beach also infers too much nobility in Frederick Henry, assuming apparently that Frederick weighs the bad (the War) against the good (Catherine's love) and chooses the good, when actually Frederick is forced out of the war effort by the battle police and his ''unauthorized'' escape from them, and is left with nothing except Catherine.

My point is that Frederick, from the time he begins to love Catherine, while he is a patient in the Milan hospital—by which time Catherine has, with Frederick's assistance, completed her own psychological recovery and come to realize that she loves him, too—has the choice of continuing his role in the slaughterous war exercise or of abandoning that exercise for the love that Catherine offers. And Catherine's devotion is noble. It is peculiar that her devotion, her willingness to give herself, has come in for so much criticism. Otto Friedrich, among others, says, ''The nothingness of Catherine Barkley was finally expressed in her announcement that 'there isn't any me. I'm you.' ''[18] Such critics seem to pass lightly over the mental state Catherine has evolved from. She has moved from a condition of near psychological destruction to a condition of balance and love.

These critics also overlook a basic psychological principle, one always generally understood but recently documented by Dr. Raymond Moody, Jr., the physician who has studied hundreds of persons who approached but were pulled back from the brink of death. Moody found that one of the most common modes of behavior following recovery is an exceptionally deep commitment to loving other people and to giving of self on their behalf: "There is remarkable agreement in the 'lessons,' as it were, which have been brought back from these close encounters with death. Almost everyone has stressed the importance in this life of trying to cultivate love for others, a love of a unique and profound kind."[19] This is precisely what Catherine has gone through psychologically (facing death) and precisely what she does, following that experience, in her relationship with Frederick (giving herself completely on his behalf).

One of the critics who comes closest to being right about Catherine is Naomi Grant, who claims that Catherine is more mature than Frederick and that she helps mature Frederick into a code of love.[20] Catherine, like other Hemingway women, is a good teacher in the art of giving of self. With observations and questions like "I'll do what you want and say what you want . . . " (p. 109) and "Can I do anything to please you?" (p. 121) Catherine sounds a bit too "Total Woman" for many, certainly for many feminists, as well as for those whose fetish for "individualism" forces them to overlook the devastating feelings of competitiveness and alienation which the ethic of individualism has inspired in recent human history.

No, Catherine's vision is the right one—not Frederick Henry's. When Frederick announces, for example, that Ettore is "going to be a captain," Catherine replies noncommitally, "That should please him" (p. 130), realizing, as Frederick does not, how silly the whole military status-and-trappings syndrome is. It is the product of imagination stunted at the adolescent stage. Wyndham Lewis hit it precisely when, in speaking of war, he said that "men must either cease thinking like children and abandon such sports, or else lose their freedom for ever."[21] But critics have continued either to overlook or condemn Catherine and to focus their attention mainly on Frederick Henry and his relationship to his mission. W. M. Frohock goes so far as to say that *Farewell* "has really but one major character [Frederick]."[22] Pier Francesco Paolini says that *Farewell* is about how Frederick "struck out on his own" on "his individual adventure."[23]

But how accurate can Catherine's vision be—her perception that better things may come to one who loves than to one who wars—when at the end of the novel she dies? This question is made even more valid because there was no attempt on Hemingway's part to duck the bald consequences of her death, as he would do later in *For Whom the Bell Tolls*, when he has Robert Jordan tell Maria that, in some vague way, "as long as there is one of us, there is both of us." Catherine has had repeated premonitions of her own death and shortly before she dies, Frederick delivers his blistering statement on the unfairness and cruelty of "Them":

Now Catherine would die. That was what you did. You died. You did not know what it was about. You never had time to learn. They threw you in and told you the rules and the first time they caught you off base they killed you. Or they killed you gratuitously like Aymo. Or gave you the syphilis like Rinaldi. But they killed you in the end. You could count on that. Stay around and they would kill you. [P. 388]

What Frederick says is true enough. "They" *do* kill you. But this does not prevent human beings from working with unrestricted vigor in trying to improve the *odds*, whether through nutrition and medical research and practices or simply through the avoidance of unnecessarily dangerous activities. Nor does it prevent people from capturing the pleasures available to them, from loving, raising children, joking with friends. Catherine's death is inevitable, as is Frederick's and our own, and its timing is finally not to be controlled. But Frederick and Catherine's love is a chance worth taking. Its possibilities for success certainly exceed those of Frederick's war mission—the kind of enterprise which human beings can have some control over, if they choose to. Arthur Waldhorn has said about Hemingway's work: "When men occasionally failed to destroy one another, nature leaped into the breach.''[24] Perhaps sensible and moral people should seek Catherine Barkley's truth: With the threat of nature so awesomely present anyway, why lower human odds against survival even further by perpetuating such destructively childish activities as war?

MARIE MORGAN

To Have and Have Not is frequently linked with *Across the River and into the Trees* as a fearful example of all that is wrong with Hemingway. Very few critics share Elliot Paul's enthusiasm for *To Have*. Paul claims that "to pay tribute to the beauty and human understanding in Hemingway's derided masterpiece would take more words than are contained in the book itself.''[25] Most share Alvah Bessie's feeling that the novel is "a vastly imperfect work,''[26] and some Delmore Schwartz's pronouncement that it "is a stupid and foolish book, a disgrace to a good writer, a book which should never have been printed.''[27]

Schwartz is excessive in his denunciation. The novel is not a good one, largely for the structural reasons usually cited (the two plots, the one featuring Harry Morgan and the one cataloging the predicaments of the people on the yachts, do not, in fact, integrate well). More unfortunate than the structural problem of the novel, however, is the way the critics have quickly adopted Harry Morgan's own interpretation of himself as a hero—carrying this odd notion considerably further than Hemingway's treatment of the character can possibly justify. Regardless of Marxist attempts to find socioeconomic awareness in the book,[28] Edgar Johnson's attempts to see Morgan as a man of "strength, tenderness, courage, ingenuity and manhood,''[29] Joseph Warren Beach's assessment of the novel as showing "some maturing process" in Hemingway,[30] even Hemingway's own pronouncement that the novel is about "the decline of the individual,''[31] it is essentially a novel about a thug, a man given almost routinely to extravagant violence.

Even Harry Morgan's rationalization for his criminal behavior, the need to support his family—an interpretation eagerly accepted by Samuel Shaw,[32] Philip Young,[33] Delmore Schwartz,[34] and others—is not at all convincing. For, while the economic effects of the Great Depression on Al Tracy's family are alluded to several times, there is no serious evidence that Harry faces such problems. Harry not only seems to have easy access to money whenever he has a need for it but also to have an affinity for criminal action. When Mr. Johnson runs out without paying Harry for the fishing charter in Cuba, Harry, without a moment's pause, turns to Mr. Sing's arrangement for smuggling alien Chinese. Johnson's perfidy seems as contrived as it is predictable. It serves as the immediate justification for a course of action that Harry seems exceptionally well-suited for anyway. Even before Harry murders Mr. Sing, he considers killing his helper, the rummy Eddy: "I was sorry for him and for what I knew I'd have to do" (p. 43).[35] The only reason Eddy is spared is that his name appears on the crew list and he would have to be accounted for. Harry, then, is casually ready to kill a man who regards him as a friend simply to keep him silent. Shortly afterward, he describes his killing of Mr. Sing:

I got his arm around behind him and came up on it but I brought it too far because I felt it go. When it went he made a funny little noise and came forward, me holding him throat and all, and bit me in the shoulder. But when I felt the arm go I dropped it. It wasn't any good to him any more and I took him by the throat with both hands, and brother, that Mr. Sing would flop just like a fish, true, his loose arm flailing. But I got him forward onto his knees and had both thumbs well in behind his talk-box, and I bent the whole thing back until she cracked. Don't you think you can't hear it crack, either. [Pp. 53–54]

When Eddy asks what Harry "had against" Mr. Sing which required that Harry kill him, Harry replies, "Nothing. . . . He was the easiest man to do business with I ever met" (p. 55). Furthermore, Harry later considers killing the entire boatload of Chinese that he is smuggling—all for twelve hundred dollars. Wyndham Lewis has said that Hemingway's violence is "deadly matter-of-fact,'' [36] a point well illustrated by Harry Morgan. More than any major character in Hemingway, Morgan conforms to psychiatrist Eric Berne's perceptive definition of a Fascist as one who ''has no respect for living tissue.'' [37] Linked with his inherent cruelty, however—and particularly germane to this study— is Harry's sense of ''mission,'' the requirement of supporting his family which merely masks his more basic need, to prove that he has *cojones*.

Hemingway's men are frequently segregated into two categories, as Lincoln Kirstein separates them: ''those with balls and those without.'' [38] It is Harry Morgan's need to prove himself a man ''with'' that forces him to develop the construct that his family's economic well-being requires him to take the chances that he does in performing the illegal and dangerous acts which he repeatedly does. His mission is to run aliens, booze, and guns; to have a fast boat; to have ready access to money; to satisfy his wife sexually, as Edmund Wilson says, ''on the scale of a Paul Bunyan'' [39]—in short, to embody the ''traditional'' characteristics of being a ''man.'' One of Harry's most vulnerable areas— and Hemingway's, too—is challenge to his manhood. When Beelips, sensing that Harry is about to withdraw from the plan to take the revolutionaries to Cuba following the bank robbery, challenges Harry with ''I thought you had *cojones*,'' Harry retorts, ''I got *cojones*. Don't you worry about my *cojones*'' (p. 109)—and Harry shows no further signs of pulling out of the venture.

Both the challenge and the response on the issue of *cojones* are as adolescent as the challenge proves to be effective. Shortly before the run to Cuba with the revolutionaries, Harry articulates what has been apparent all along, that he measures himself almost entirely by the evidence of his own *cojones*. At Freddy's Bar, in a rush of self-pity, Harry says to himself: ''Where's the money coming from to keep Marie and the girls? I've got no boat, no cash, I got no education. What can a one-armed man work at? All I've got is my *cojones* to peddle'' (p. 147). In fact, Harry is secretly delighted in this position. Though he has done virtually nothing throughout the novel *except* peddle his *cojones* (even before he lost his boat and his arm, even when he had cash, and despite the facts that he knows Marie can take care of herself and that he cares nothing for his daughters anyway), Harry can now rationalize what he ''must do'' on the basis of his ''duty'' rather than as a series of palliatives for his insecure sexual ego, his ''manhood''—what Edmund Wilson calls ''a choral refrain of praise of his *cojones*.''[40]

Where does Marie fit into the scheme of Harry's life? Her role, like Catherine Barkley's, is to represent an alternative vision. She plays love-admiration-giving-domesticity to Harry's violence-cruelty-taking-''manhood.'' Since, for all his talk of ''no honest money in boats anymore,'' Harry shows virtually no evidence of trying to earn money honestly, the issue of money becomes effectively moot, leaving Harry with two available lifestyle choices, love and humanity with Marie, or mission and inhumanity with his *cojones*. He, of course, chooses the latter. But what are the possibilities with Marie? When Marie and the domestic life are introduced, Harry says: ''That night I was sitting in the living room smoking a cigar and drinking a whiskey and water and listening to Gracie Allen on the radio. The girls had gone to the show and sitting there I felt sleepy and I felt good'' (p. 64). Later:

Lying still in the bed he felt her lips on his face and searching for him and then her hand on him and he rolled over against her close.

''Do you want to?''

''Yes. Now.''

''I was asleep. Do you remember when we'd do it asleep?''

''Listen, do you mind the arm? Don't it make you feel funny?''

''You're silly. I like it. Any that's you I like. Put it along there. Go on. I like it, true.'' . . .

He went to sleep with the stump of his arm out wide on the pillow, and she lay for a long time looking at him. She could see his face in the street light through the window. I'm lucky, she was thinking. Those girls. They don't know what they'll get. I know what I've got and what I've had. I've been a lucky woman. Him laying like a loggerhead. I'm glad it was a arm and not a leg. Why'd he have to lose that arm? It's funny though, I don't mind. I've been a lucky woman. [Pp. 112–115]

Like Catherine Barkley (and like Maria and Renata in later novels), Marie Morgan, while certainly enjoying the physical gratification that she receives with Harry, does *give* herself completely to their relationship, and in ways other than the merely sexual—and that is something that Harry seems incapable of doing. Theodore Bardacke says, "Marie and her husband experience a real and complete relationship. There is between them a loyalty, respect, and virility that to a certain extent remain with Marie even after the death of her husband."[41] Leon Linderoth goes further: "the marital relationship between Marie and Harry is as close and complete as any the author has ever created."[42] The fact remains that, though the relationship is indeed close and satisfying, Harry allows it to become only a small part of his life. There is little reason to assume that he thinks about it very much.

Marie tries to substitute what she offers Harry for the "mission" lifestyle that he has chosen. When Harry is preparing his machine gun for the Cuba trip, she says, "Don't take that"; and she asks, "Honey, you aren't going on that kind of trip?"; and still later exclaims, "Oh God, I wish you didn't have to do these things" (p. 127)—and Hemingway never demonstrates that Harry *does* have "to do these things." Harry's lament, "What chance have I to enjoy my home?" (p. 127) is as thin and unconvincing as his earlier assertion about the Cuban venture: "I didn't ask for any of this and if you've got to do it you've got to do it" (p. 105). Harry loves what he is doing, with its danger and excitement, with its element of intrigue, with, above all else, the sense of self-esteem and "manhood" that such missions inspire in him.

There is considerable irony, as well as hypocrisy, incidentally, in the way Harry Morgan views the indiscretions of others. On the way to Cuba after the robbery Harry appears to accept the Cuban boy's interpretation of Roberto as "a good revolutionary but a bad man" (p. 158). He fails to see that he, Harry, is also a "bad man" with what he has convinced himself is a good cause. Later, after hearing the boy's explanation of the revolutionary cause, Harry rather righteously thinks to himself,

"He's a radical. . . . That's what he is, a radical" (p. 166)—
a peculiar sort of righteousness for one who is so casual about
killing other men.

There is irony, too, in the attempt of two generations of critics to make philosophical statements, *writ large*, of Harry Morgan's values in contrast with those of the yacht people and of
Harry's dying statement that "No matter how a man alone ain't
got no bloody fucking chance" (p. 225). It is easy enough to
observe the alcoholism-homosexuality-masturbation (read: moral
decay) of the yacht set; and, indeed, there are some excellent
"social-consciousness" passages, such as the one revealing the
grain broker's thoughts about people he has ruined:

He would not need to worry about what he had done to other people, nor what had happened to them due to him, nor how they'd ended;
who'd moved from houses on the Lake Shore drive to taking boarders
out in Austin, whose debutante daughters now were dentists' assistants
when they had a job; who ended up a night watchman at sixty-three
after that last corner; who shot himself early one morning before
breakfast and which one of his children found him, and what the mess
looked like; who now rode on the L to work, when there was work,
from Berwyn, trying to sell, first bonds; then motor cars; then house-
to-housing novelties and specialties (we don't want no peddlers, get
out of here, the door slammed in his face) until he varied the leaning
drop his father made from forty-two floors up, with no rush of plumes
as when an eagle falls, to a step forward onto the third rail in front of
the Aurora-Elgin train, his overcoat pocket full of un-saleable combi-
nation eggbeaters and fruit juice extracters. *Just let me demonstrate it,
madame. You attach it here, screw down on this little gadget here.
Now watch.* No, I don't want it. *Just try one.* I don't want it. Get
out. . . .
Some made the long drop from the apartment or the office window;
some took it quietly in two-car garages with the motor running; some
used the native tradition of the Colt or Smith and Wesson; those well-
constructed implements that end insomnia, terminate remorse, cure
cancer, avoid bankruptcy, and blast an exit from intolerable positions
by the pressure of a finger; those admirable American instruments so
easily carried, so sure of effect, so well designed to end the American

dream when it becomes a nightmare, their only drawback the mess they leave for relatives to clean up.

The men he broke made all these various exits but that never worried him. Somebody had to lose and only suckers worried. [Pp. 237–38]

The problem is that, when critics like Joseph Warren Beach explain that the presence of the yacht people is "to set off in higher relief the essential manliness of Harry Morgan,"[43] they conspire to mute Morgan's viciousness. It is hardly more reprehensible to masturbate, to have homosexual affairs, even to be responsible for the suicide of others than casually to crush the throats of criminal business associates or to plan the murder of one's friends. Such critics fail to make significant enough the fact that, because of the lack of integration of the two plots, the "moral decay" of the yacht people does not confirm anything about Harry anyway. It is similarly unfortunate for Pier Francesco Paolini to observe Harry Morgan's "man alone" words and say of Hemingway that "it had taken him a lifetime to learn them,"[44] as though this "condemnation of individualism" were Hemingway's new vision, something that neither this novel nor subsequent Hemingway works confirm. For, unlike *The Grapes of Wrath*, where there is a gradual and convincing working out of the social ethic that individuals must join together to survive, in *To Have and Have Not*, Harry's entire life—and even his death, except for that one pronouncement—is devoted to a celebration of individual man and the "missions" he creates to demonstrate his own *cojones*.

Elliot Paul, the foremost defender of *To Have and Have Not*, is probably right (though he seems unaware of the tragedy implicit in his analysis) when he says that Harry Morgan "has the qualities which characterized the builders of this nation in happier days. He is strong and courageous, ambitious and proud. Men respect and fear him. He lets nothing stand in his way."[45] "Happier days" aside, Harry is certainly all of that—and like those nation builders, he is cruel, selfish, and profiteering, though

he remains decidedly bush-league beside the Goulds, the Van-
derbilts, and similar notorious robber barons. Whether the ethic
is called "progress," "rugged individualism," or "the American Dream," the ethic embodies the wrong vision of the kind
of social and psychological investment that people should make
in each other. Like the earlier "individualists," Harry is a *taker*,
though a greater investment of himself in the lifestyle that Hemingway created in the character of Marie could have taught him
better.

MARIA

As with *A Farewell to Arms* and *To Have and Have Not*, some
rather notable critics have said some fairly silly things about *For
Whom the Bell Tolls*. In my judgment this is, at least technically, Hemingway's greatest novel. It was exceptionally popular, outselling all other American novels except *Gone with the
Wind* during the several years following its publication.[46] Mark
Schorer has claimed it "is no *War and Peace*"[47]—whatever that
may mean. W. M. Frohock says Hemingway wrote *For Whom*
"with Hollywood production and even possibly a specific Hollywood actor in mind"[48]—the kind of observation that is fairly
easy to make after a novel has been made into a movie. Dwight
Macdonald, in his clever critical parody of Hemingway's style,
says of the novels generally and of this period of Hemingway's
career specifically: "Most of the tricks were good tricks and they
worked fine for a while especially in the short stories. Ernest
was stylish in the hundred-yard dash but he didn't have the wind
for the long stuff. . . . After 1930, he just didn't have it any
more. His legs began to go and his syntax became boring and
the critics began to ask why he didn't put in a few subordinate
clauses just to make it look good."[49]

As they did with Catherine Barkley, the critics almost uniformly turned thumbs-down on the character of Maria. Theodore Bardacke says Hemingway "recreated Catherine Barkley
in the form of Maria, with one important difference—her political convictions. Maria is submissive and without individual

personality; altogether, as Edmund Wilson pointed out, an 'amoebic' creature."[50] Maxwell Geismar claims "Maria is on the whole more theatrical than substantial. She is a sort of compendium of the virtues of the modern proletarian mistress."[51] Sharon Dean pronounces Maria "more a symbol than a person."[52] And Samuel Shaw says: "Maria does not come through with the clear definition of the others. She is the Hemingway woman, living to serve the physical and emotional needs of her man, romanticized beyond anything in earlier novels."[53]

Here it is again: *the* "Hemingway woman"—mindless, vapid, passive, symbolic/allegorical, pathetically submissive. All these assessments are in large part misdirected, if not simply wrong, and for two reasons. First, as with Catherine Barkley, these critics measure Maria's behavior against what they perceive as "normal" behavior (individualistic, aggressive, acquisitive), failing to realize that such behavior patterns are usually altered radically, as physician Raymond Moody, Jr., found,[54] in those who brush close to physical (or psychological) death. Most persons having such traumatic experiences learn what, in "better times," they cannot see—that alienating oneself from other human beings, through some ethic of "individualism," is a lonely and self-destructive enterprise; that being personally or professionally "aggressive" at the expense of others is rarely ennobling; and that the acquisition of goods, prestige, or power is a pursuit which looks exceptionally silly to one facing death.

Why does the dying person enjoy looking at new spring grass? Or being with persons that he or she cares for? Most of the enterprises with which people occupy their lives are basically the enterprises of children (adolescents at best), proving that they are independent of their parents, and later of people generally; proving that they can "get ahead," "stand out," "make it on their own"; proving, through aggressive personal relationships, business practices, belligerence, and other hurtful activities that they, like Hemingway and his heroes, have *cojones*. Catherine Barkley confronts psychological death (and is restored by the unwitting assistance of Frederick Henry). Maria confronts both physical death at the hands of the Fascists and psychological death as a consequence of her brutal treatment (and is restored by the joint therapeutic efforts of Pilar and Robert Jordan). Like nearly all of the hundreds of subjects of Dr. Moody who confronted death but were restored to life, Catherine and Maria find a new sense of proportion about "essential things" which few who do not share that kind of trauma seem able to develop. These new-found commitments to love other people, to give of self, to merge with others, represent life's "essential things."

The second reason that the generally negative critical assess-ments of Maria are unfortunate is that, by repudiating Maria and, by extension, the love ethic that she represents, the critics are left in the unrewarding position of implicitly endorsing the futile "mission" ethic of Robert Jordan. His is a territorial ethic (about someone else's territory), the cyclic silliness of which is well reflected by Jordan's beginning and ending the novel lying on the ground in similar positions of vigilance. Nothing of moral consequence has occurred between the two scenes, for all his efforts.

Jordan's sense of mission is abundantly evident throughout the novel, and the success of the mission—the preservation of the Spanish "territory" for the Loyalists who claim it as legally theirs—remains more important than anything else, including his own life ("he did not give any importance to what happened to himself" p. 4).[55] At this point in the story Jordan can, perhaps with justification, feel that his task is significant, for General Golz has told him that "the attack" cannot be successful unless the bridge is blown up and at precisely the right time: "That is the only road on which they can bring up reinforcements. That is the only road on which they can get up tanks, or artillery, or even move a truck toward the pass which I attack. I must know that bridge is gone" (p. 5). From the importance which Golz attaches to the bridge mission and from Jordan's commitment to the Loyalist cause, Jordan gradually comes to believe naively that "that bridge can be the point on which the future of the human race can turn" (p. 43). This belief is soon eroded when he comes to realize that the Fascists know of the attack plan in advance and when he learns that the level of atrocities perpetrated by the Fascists is hardly distinguishable from that perpetrated by the Loyalists, whom he has automatically taken to be the representatives of good in the conflict.

Jordan's allegiance to his "duty" comes at considerable moral cost to himself. Near the beginning, during a conversation with Anselmo, Jordan explains that, like Anselmo, he *usually* does not like to kill human beings—"But I feel nothing against it when it is necessary. When it is for the cause" (p. 39). Later Jordan explains to Pilar and Santiago what happened to the earlier dynamiter, Kashkin: "I shot him. . . . He was too badly wounded to travel and I shot him" (p. 149). By this time Jordan has so internalized the soldier's power of rationalization that he can fairly casually handle the thought of the probable destruction of his new friends:

So you say that it is not that which will happen to yourself but that which may happen to the woman and the girl and to the others that you think of. All right. What would have happened to them if you had not come? What happened to them and what passed with them before you were ever here? You must not think in that way. You have no responsibility for them except in action. The orders do not come from you. They come from Golz. And who is Golz? A good general. The best you've ever served under. But should a man carry out impossible orders knowing what they lead to? Even though they come from Golz, who is the party as well as the army? Yes. He should carry them out because it is only in the performing of them that they can prove to be impossible. How do you know they are impossible until you have tried them? If every one said orders were impossible to carry out when they were received where would you be? Where would we all be if you just said, "Impossible," when orders came? [P. 162]

Though Jordan is briefly moved by reading the papers of the young Fascist he kills not far from El Sordo's camp, he is nonetheless able to shrug off the almost certain knowledge that Pablo, in order to acquire additional horses for the escape, is planning to murder all of the members of the small guerrilla band who will help them at the bridge: "I wonder what the bastard is planning now. . . . But I am pretty sure I know. Well, that is his, not mine. Thank God I do not know these new men" (p. 404).

Robert Jordan's moral culpability is compounded when, not even midway through the novel, it becomes apparent that the Fascists know of the coming "surprise" attack, which can be successful only if the enemy does *not* know it is coming. There have been rumors to that effect almost from the beginning, and, during his visit to El Sordo's camp, Jordan is told that the enemy almost certainly knows. This invalidates the entire mission. There are the added complications of the snow (which allows the Fascists to track the guerrillas, as, in fact, they do track El Sordo) and Pablo's stealing the exploder and detonators, and what emerges is not merely an impossible mission, but a stupid one as well. The stupidity is compounded as Andrés, carrying Jordan's message to Golz to stop the attack, is nearly bombed by Loyalist sentries, is arrested by Andre Marty, and realizes too late that the attack could not have been stopped, even by Golz, once the virtually uncontrollable war machine had been put into gear and released:

It is doubtful if the outcome of Andrés's mission would have been any different if he and Gomez had been allowed to proceed without Andre Marty's hindrance. There was no one at the front with sufficient authority to cancel the attack. The machinery had been in motion much too long for it to be stopped suddenly now. There is a great inertia about all military operations of any size. But once this inertia has been overcome and movement is under way they are almost as hard to arrest as to initiate. [P. 423]

What is the human cost of dynamiting the bridge, a mission Maxwell Geismar describes as "hardly a creative act to begin with,"[56] a mission which, because it is part of an attack plan now doomed to certain failure, no longer has any validity whatever, except perhaps to prove that Robert Jordan, too, has *cojones*, or to demonstrate what Philip Young interprets as Jordan's (and implicitly Hemingway's) "attraction toward death"?[57] The close-at-hand human toll includes the slaughter of El Sordo's band, Fernando shot in the groin, Eladio shot in the head, Anselmo killed by flying steel from the explosion of the bridge, Pablo murdering the assisting guerrillas (an act made simpler apparently because "they were not of our band," p. 456), the killing of a sprinkling of Fascists in the mountains and at the bridge, and the implicit death of Robert Jordan.

Many critics have joined Robert Jordan in trying to find a noble interpretation for his fruitless military venture. The Russian critic Ivan Kashkeen, for example, makes the strange assertion that Jordan dies "in fulfillment of a moral duty."[58] W. M. Frohock says of Jordan and his relationship with Maria, "love is the sweeter for having to be swallowed up in death."[59] Mimi Gladstein, apparently accepting at face value Jordan's maudlin "As-long-as-there-is-one-of-us,-there-is-both-of-us" pronouncement to Maria, implies that somehow Jordan's death does not count as much because "Maria is Robert's individual share in immortality."[60] Lionel Trilling is much more on the mark when he says: "Hemingway knows that his hero must die in *some* moral circumstance; he lamely and belatedly contrives for Robert Jordan a problem of—courage. And so we get what we all like, and rightly like, a good fighting death, but in the face of all that Jordan's death truly signifies, this is devastatingly meaningless."[61]

Robert Jordan's death need not have occurred at all. Putting aside the pointless fact that Jordan need not have joined the Loyalist cause to begin with, he, like Frederick Henry and Harry Morgan, has two courses of action (actually visions about human life and "essential things") from which to choose. Like the others, he opts for "duty," "courage," "loyalty"—in short, he chooses mission over love. W. M. Frohock and others are wrong when they make such claims as "The characters are caught in a box from which there is no exit except through the inevitable violent catastrophe."[62] There is the exit which Frederick Henry was forced into, and which Robert Jordan was free at any time to choose, the exit of the "separate peace," the turning away from a venture which could only be as destructive as it would be fruitless, away from bureaucratic stupidity and insensitivity, toward the deeply personal experience of love and commitment which Maria represents—difficult as such a choice may sound to a world with national, racial-ethnic, and socioeconomic territories which, so the mythology of human territoriality goes, must be defended at whatever cost whenever political and military "experts" claim that such action is vital to some group's "interest."

Despite Mark Schorer's observation that Maria is "that perfect sexual creature of the private Hemingway mythology,"[63] and Philip Young's claim that "Maria is just too ethereal for the world she is in,"[64] I must point out that Maria's truth, her capacity to give herself fully in love, surpasses what Golz's, Marty's, even Pablo's truths offer Robert Jordan. Robert and Maria's first night together in the sleeping bag—not such an unusual sexual arrangement, despite Leslie Fiedler's somewhat righteous pronouncements about it[65]—marks the development of a possible alternative course of action for Robert Jordan. When Pilar, in interrogating Jordan shortly after his early sexual experience with Maria, asks if he cares for the girl, Jordan replies, "Yes. Suddenly and very much" (p. 91). When, during a subsequent experience, Jordan "felt the earth move out and away from under them" (p. 159), he is describing a sensation which transcends orgasm alone. It is a sensation that gains its power from a merging of love with sexual energy—the kind of intense experience which, if Pilar is to be believed, few people ever know (p. 175).

The specialness of his feelings for Maria and his growing awareness that the Fascists know about the attack plan should, one would think, cause Jordan to reconsider his whole-hearted allegiance to his mission. Such a reconsideration would seem to be increasingly in order as the relationship deepens and Maria begins the kind of complete giving of self that Catherine Barkley and Marie Morgan have offered before her. Maria says: "If I am to be thy woman I should please thee in all ways" (p. 160); "I am thee and thou art me and all of one is the other" (p. 262); "But we will be one now and there will never be a separate one. . . . I will be thee when thou art not there. Oh, I love thee so and I must care well for thee" (p. 263).

Perhaps it is the intensity of Maria's pronouncements on love that causes some critics essentially to misread the significance of the relationship between mission and love in *For Whom the Bell Tolls*. Robert Spiller wrongly says "it is in the intense and physical love for a woman of his kind rather than in self-sacrifice for a cause that Jordan finds his reasons for life and for death."[66] Sharon Dean, equally wrong, says that Jordan "progresses to the realization that love is dominant over work and so can be felt even during the crisis of blowing a bridge."[67] In response to Maria's most noble of human ethics (espoused by Socrates, by Jesus, and by the distinct minority of decent and loving men and women throughout the centuries), Jordan does not offer love and selflessness in return. Despite his professions of love and talk of marriage and Missoula, he offers instead a uselessly demolished bridge, a handful of dead Fascists, and a substantially larger number of dead friends—an ethic succinctly captured when he tells the sleeping Maria, "We'll be killed but we'll blow the bridge" (p. 371).

RENATA

In the canon of commentary on Hemingway's fiction, without question the most creative denunciations have been reserved for *Across the River and into the Trees*, and for its hero, Colonel Cantwell, and its heroine, Renata. Despite Hemingway's own feeling that the novel was better than *A Farewell to Arms*,[68] perhaps the best that he had ever written,[69] critics have uniformly felt otherwise. Michael Moloney calls it "slight and flaccid";[70] Maxwell Geismar says "it is not only Hemingway's worst novel; it is a synthesis of everything that is bad in his previous work and it throws a doubtful light on the future."[71] Geismar goes on to say of the novel's hero: Cantwell "is a caricature of such figures as the Lieutenant Henry of *A Farewell to Arms* or the Jake of *The Sun Also Rises*."[72] Jackson Benson says that "Cantwell is in part Hemingway romanticizing his own position, mourning his own middle age, and sentimentalizing his continued desperate concern for virility."[73] And Renata, like Catherine Barkley and Maria, is consistently scorned as shallow, "unbelievable," and "forced."

There are not many solid features to point to in *Across the River*. The tone *is* mawkish. The dialogue *is* contrived. Cantwell *is* very nearly a caricature. There is a general oddness about the relationship between the aging soldier and the teenage girl who is so fascinated by his crippled hand (part of what Frederick Hoffman describes as "an almost obsessive preoccupation with wounds and death").[74] For all its frailty, however, the novel once again sets up a moral dichotomy between a male sense of mission and a female sense of love. Once more (despite Hemingway's personal preference for "mission") the moral scale tips clearly in favor of the love-giving vision of the heroine, who, in addition to her small role as lover, serves more directly than any previous Hemingway character as psychotherapist.

Cantwell certainly needs therapy. He is a man with a much-troubled mind and three days to live, a man whose heart condition makes it necessary for him to "soup up" so high on nitroglycerin that his doctor tells him, "They ought to make you drag a chain like a high-octane truck" (p. 9).[75] Cantwell cannot reconcile his imminent death with the catalog of his destructive mistakes as a professional soldier. For all his pretense about the pleasures of Venice, of bird shooting and of drinking and talking with old friends such as the Gran Maestro, Cantwell cannot dismiss from his mind his own mortality nor the flood of horrible memories which make that mortality even more difficult to face. As he crosses the Piave River on his way to Venice, he remembers the fighting that he experienced there and the abortive attempt to dispose of the war dead:

There had been a great killing at the last of the offensive and someone, to clear the river bank positions and the road in the hot weather, had ordered the dead thrown into the canals. Unfortunately, the canal gates were still in the Austrians' hands down the river, and they were closed.

So there was little movement to the water, and the dead had stayed there a long time, floating and bloating face up and face down regardless of nationality until they had attained colossal proportions. Finally, after organization had been established, labor troops hauled them out at night and buried them close to the road. The Colonel looked for added greenness close to the road but could not note any. [Pp. 20–21]

He remembers, too, that, during the winter, "with a bad sore throat, he had killed men who came, wearing stick bombs hooked up on a harness under their shoulders with the heavy, calf hide packs and the bucket helmets. They were the enemy" (p. 32). He later recalls the costly campaign to reach Grosshau:

We met a truck at this place and slowed up, and he had the usual gray face and he said, "Sir, there is a dead GI in the middle of the road up ahead, and every time any vehicle goes through they have to run over him, and I'm afraid it is making a bad impression on the troops."
"We'll get him off the road."
So we got him off the road.
And I remember just how he felt, lifting him, and how he had been flattened and the strangeness of his flatness.
Then there was one other thing, I remember. We had put an awful lot of white phosphorus on the town before we got in for good, or whatever you would call it. That was the first time I ever saw a German dog eating a roasted German kraut. Later on I saw a cat working on him too. It was a hungry cat, quite nice looking, basically. You wouldn't think a good German cat would eat a good German soldier, would you Daughter? Or a good German dog eat a good German soldier's ass which had been roasted by white phosphorus. [Pp. 256–57]

The list of bad memories goes on: the loss of huge numbers of lives, including three battalions which Cantwell himself "lost," because of someone's wrong decisions; the consistent and destructive lies of military leaders such as Patton, as well as Cantwell's own "four" lies; the 122 men that Cantwell has personally killed, "not counting possibles" (p. 123); the more than 140,000 Allied troops that Cantwell saw killed in a single year;

the generals running the war from secure trailers in the rear, with maps, colored pencils, and plenty of bourbon; the ridiculous orders that he and others willingly carried out ("But you get the orders, and you have to carry them out," p. 188); the experience of being bombed by mistake by Allied planes.

Add to these memories the new revelations of the boatman about his family and the war ("We were six. We lost two beyond the Isonzo, one on the Bainsizza and one on the Carso. Then we lost this brother I speak of on the Grappa and I remained" p. 47) and of the waiter who no longer has a wife and children ("Your mediums smacked our house in Treviso" p. 150). Consider, finally, the most significant of Cantwell's realizations, revealed to Renata in response to her observations about the Germans ("But they were in the wrong" p. 122). Cantwell replies, "Of course. But who has not been?" and "When we have killed so many we can afford to be kind" (pp. 122–123), in effect acknowledging, as Frederick Henry and Robert Jordan had before him, that the level of morality (perhaps more accurately, immorality) as he observed it was almost indistinguishable between the two sides. There was a lack of sensitivity and justice on both sides that invalidated the nobility of their missions. There was untold human suffering on both sides caused by men like Cantwell who unquestioningly carried out the foolish and devastating orders of others.

Cantwell, however, for all his verbalizing about atrocities and the mental discomfort which they cause him, and for all his cheap talk about leaving the military life ("I'm going to chuck the army and live in this town, very simply, on my retirement pay" p. 127)—especially cheap since he knows he is dying—like the earlier Hemingway heroes thrives on his role as a soldier and the image he projects. He reminds Jackson to call him "Sir"; he leaves a "monument" to himself at the site of his wounding; he reminds the couple in the bar that his uniform deserves respect. Though, later in the novel, he shows some awareness of the childishness of his image and accoutrements, when he says to himself, "put on your soldier suit" (p. 180), he puts it on, and with more than a little pride.

Throughout his career, Cantwell has well illustrated the principle of human behavior articulated by Simone Weil: "When you know it is possible to kill without blame or punishment, you kill; or at least you lavish encouraging smiles on those who kill. If by chance you feel a little disgust, you keep quiet about it and soon you stifle it, for fear of appearing to lack manliness."[76] Manliness, however, has become a peripheral issue with Cantwell because of the imminence of his death. When a critic like Mimi Gladstein says, "Colonel Cantwell returns to scenes of military triumph to try to regain a sense of manhood,"[77] she overlooks the fact that Cantwell's military memories in the novel are primarily those of destruction and gloom, not of triumph, and the fact that, except for long-established behavior, speech, and dress habits which illustrate "manhood," Cantwell has returned to Venice and the surrounding countryside as a dying person might walk over a familiar meadow or down a familiar street, to see things "one last time," firmly to place familiar scenes, people, and memories in their final positions in his mind.

This retrospection explains why Samuel Shaw and others find the love scenes in *Across the River* awkward or "posed."[78] The novel is about love, yes, but not about love-making, as were the earlier Hemingway novels (the fumbling episode in the gondola is only incidental to the plot). Renata's love consists in giving Cantwell a psychological peace which he cannot achieve for himself. Renata knows from early on that Cantwell is dying; she asks, "But how would you like to be a girl nineteen years old in love with a man over fifty years old that you knew was going to die?" (p. 91). Like the strange early dialogue between Catherine Barkley and Frederick Henry in *A Farewell to Arms*, Cantwell and Renata say some peculiar things to each other once they openly acknowledge that Cantwell is dying:

"Maybe I am wrong. But we're having fun again and whatever the bad thing was is gone now."

"It's gone the way the mist is burned off the hollows in broken ground when the sun comes out," the Colonel said. "And you're the sun."

"I want to be the moon, too."

"You are," the Colonel told her. "Also any particular planet that you wish to be and I will give you an accurate location of the planet. Christ, Daughter, you can be a God-damn constellation if you like. Only that's an airplane."

"I'll be the moon. She has many troubles too."

"Yes. Her sorrows come regularly. But she always fills before she wanes."

"She looks so sad to me sometimes across the Canal that I cannot stand it."

"She's been around a long time," the Colonel said. . . .

"Ettore, two Montgomerys, super Montgomerys, with garlic olives, not the big ones, and please call the home of this lady and let her know when you have completed the communication. And all of this as rapidly as possible."

"Yes, my Colonel."

"Now, Daughter, let us resume the having of the fun."

"It was resumed when you spoke," she said. [Pp. 99–101]

The language is formal and intentionally diversionary, but, as in Catherine's case, it reflects the beginning of psychotherapy. It is the awkwardly transitional verbal stage which must come between the acknowledgment of coming death and serious discussion designed to make that death easier for the individual facing it. It is not psychotherapy of a dispassionate kind; it is psychotherapy set in an environment of love and giving similar to the environments created by Catherine Barkley, Marie Morgan, and the Spanish Maria. When Renata tells Cantwell in the gondola that they are in their "home," she is pointing out that the love-sharing-domesticity ethic is itself a "moveable feast"—though unfortunately it is one which, while permanent for the Hemingway heroines, serves only as a respite for Hemingway's heroes before they move on to their more important missions.

Cantwell represents the first Hemingway novelistic hero to outlive all his missions and to find himself facing death without the odd kind of comfort which the mission milieu seems to provide for other Hemingway heroes facing death. There is no more duty, no more bravery, no more causes—nothing, in fact, between Cantwell and a very disordered death except the therapeutic instincts of the young Renata. Her instincts are good. Though she later tells him that she does not like his "business," his "sad trade," she at first tells Cantwell, "I love you to be in your trade and I love you" (p. 114), not because she believes what she says but because one does not undermine a dying person's confidence in his life-long beliefs. This removes too abruptly what may be a critical support at a time when the most support is badly needed.

Instead, Renata helps Cantwell to adjust his perceptions about his mission-oriented life, without destroying his life's beliefs by telling him they are wrong. Thus he can die with as much peace as possible. Renata gently forces Cantwell to explain the memories that trouble him most, and works up to the question, "What is your greatest sorrow?" to which Cantwell replies, "Other people's orders" (p. 210). Shortly afterward, Cantwell realizes what Renata is trying to achieve, and sensing the solace she may be able to provide his tormented mind, cooperatively asks, "What would you like to know, Daughter?" When she replies, "Everything," he says, "All right. . . . Here goes" (p. 220). For the next few hours, Cantwell relates, in effect, his life, including a diatribe against air power (ironic morality when one considers that the infantry does the same thing, only less efficiently) and the details of his lost regiment. At one point Renata asks, "Don't you see you need to tell me things to purge your bitterness?" (p. 240); with that urging, Cantwell pursues his story to the end, continues musing, in fact, even when he sees that Renata has fallen asleep. Among his most significant observations are his comments about death:

Death is a lot of shit, he thought. It comes to you in small fragments that hardly show where it has entered. It comes, sometimes, atrociously. It can come from unboiled water; an un-pulled-up mosquito boot, or it can come with the great, white-hot, clanging roar we have lived with. It comes in small cracking whispers that precede the noise of the automatic weapon. It can come with the smoke-emitting arc of the grenade, or the sharp, cracking drop of the mortar. [Pp. 219–20]

Ironically, most of the causes of death enumerated are man-made. It is a natural cause, however, his failing heart, which is soon to cause Cantwell's death, as it is a natural cause, unsuccessful childbirth, which causes Catherine Barkley's. To some extent Cantwell and the Gran Maestro are right when they lament that "everyone is hurt" (pp. 122–23), as is Frederick Henry when he says that "They kill you." Having said that, however, one must decide whether living is worth the effort; if we decide in the positive, then we have affirmed that the experience is worth the cost. Once having concluded this, it seems to me that we have nothing less than a moral obligation to "make it work," at least within our own environment and to whatever extent we can exert control over those elements near us which would make it *not* work. Theologian Jack Mendelsohn puts it particularly well when he says:

Like all other humans, I live on borrowed time. I never know when my string of time will run out. I have no way of anticipating what tragedies may befall me at the next step, the next ring of the telephone, the next rising of the sun. My notion of religious fulfillment is to learn how to accept this fate with a ringing affirmation of all that makes life worth living. Religion is my inspiration to be a creative, cooperative human being in spite of the fact that life may crush me at any moment and death blot me out. As a skeptic, I cannot comfort myself with supernatural promises. I know that human existence contains its irreducible elements of tragedy and incompleteness. . . . For me, the fundamental question of life is not "why" but "how." How shall I live while I live?[79]

Such a commitment requires that individuals "invest" themselves heavily in other people rather than turn their energies exclusively outward toward careers, or, worse, toward abstractions such as religious dogma or political or national ideologies, usually to the detriment of their relationships with people that they love, or could love. Psychiatrist Eric Berne puts it more bluntly when he says that he is mainly concerned about the "trash" in people's lives, which he defines as "things people do instead of saying Hello"[80]—the numberless activities people commit themselves to in lieu of committing themselves to each other. The missions of Cantwell and other Hemingway heroes well illustrate Berne's concept of "trash." They give their energies—and often their lives—for inflated or manufactured causes which they mislead themselves into thinking are worth not only their lives but the lives of countless others who may share no interest in the causes at all. They have the mission-territorial vision of the KKK, the KGB, and other acquisitive despots, none of which is committed in a genuine way to a high quality of human decency or a social order formed by moral considerations.

Hemingway's women, on the other hand, especially the important ones like Catherine Barkley, Marie Morgan, Maria, and Renata, reject the death-seeking mentality of the hero with whom each is associated. Instead they offer an alternative—a life-affirming—vision of people and their relationships. They try (like Cassandra, with notable lack of success) to share that vision with their men, urging them to sweep away the "trash" in their lives. What could remain, they prophesy hopelessly, are the "essential things," the relatively simple fundamentals of love and giving on a personal level—a noble gift, it seems to me, to members of a misson-minded civilization which may not have much time remaining to correct itself.

III

Bitches and Other Simplistic Assumptions

Just as Catherine Barkley, Marie Morgan, Maria, and Renata are generally considered mindless and subservient sex creatures (Marie somewhat less than the others), so conventional critical wisdom tells us that Brett Ashley, Margot Macomber, Helen ("The Snows of Kilimanjaro"), and Dorothy Bridges are Hemingway's bitch-women. Because critical wisdom is often largely the perpetuation of "party lines" of interpretation, however, I would point out that the "bitch" designation has been far too glibly attached to the four women in question here, that all of these so-called bitches are considerably more complicated than the label implies, and, most important, that some of the women—including the infamous Margot Macomber—are actually morally superior to the male characters with whom they are associated and by whom, in large part, they are judged.

BRETT ASHLEY

Like other Hemingway heroines, Brett Ashley has been denounced as a weak character. Allen Tate has called her "false," and has claimed that she is more caricature than character.[1] Edwin Muir has claimed that Brett "is the sentimentally regarded dare-devil, and she never becomes real."[2] The more serious and frequent critical charges against Brett Ashley, however, are that she lacks the characteristics of a woman and, worse, that she is a "bitch." On the first charge, Theodore Bardacke claims that Brett is a "woman devoid of womanhood."[3] Jackson Benson says that Brett is "a female who never becomes a woman."[4] Mimi Gladstein says that Brett has a "bisexual image."[5] And, the most pointed, Pamella Farley calls Brett "a perversion of femininity."[6] (Much has been made lately, incidentally, based on "quick studies" of Hemingway's unpublished manuscripts, of Hemingway's own alleged bisexuality and general confusion of sex roles, and, given the contemporary preoccupation with such matters, much more is surely going to be said about it.)[7]

A careful reading of *The Sun Also Rises*, however—the only one of his books that Hemingway was almost completely satisfied with[8]—reveals that Brett was an individual whose female sexual appeal and general attractiveness were exceptional, despite her bobbed hair and her occasional association with homosexuals. From the beginning of the book, men find her irresistible. When Jake, as narrator, first introduces Brett, he says, "Brett was damned good-looking. She wore a slipover jersey sweater and a tweed skirt, and her hair was brushed back like a boy's. She started all that [that is, the new female hairstyle]. She was built with curves like the hull of a racing yacht, and you missed none of it with that wool jersey" (p. 22).[9] Robert Cohn, too, is immediately captivated by Brett, and a short time later, he says, "She's a remarkably attractive woman" (p. 38).

Every significant male character in the novel at one time or another comments on Brett's female attractiveness. When he is introduced to Brett, Bill Gorton says, "Beautiful lady" (p. 74), and later he says, "She's damned nice" (p. 76). Mike Campbell says, "Brett, you *are* a lovely piece. Don't you think she's beautiful?" (p. 79)—a refrain that he reiterates through the rest of the novel. There are Jake's repeated narrative descriptions: "Brett wore a black, sleeveless evening dress. She looked quite beautiful" (p. 146) and "Brett was radiant" (p. 207) and, finally, the near-uncontrollable infatuation of the nineteen-year-old bullfighter, Pedro Romero, for Brett. Hemingway makes amply clear, in short, that this is an exceptionally appealing woman—bright, beautiful, and sexual—and to call Brett "non-feminine," or "bisexual," or a "perversion of femininity," is to measure her by a standard of "womanhood" which is confining indeed.

A more unfortunate and inaccurate form of party-line criticism on Brett Ashley, however, is that which glibly labels her a "bitch." This assessment apparently began with Edmund Wilson and his interpretation of Brett Ashley as "an exclusively destructive force,"[10] and has been perpetuated almost uniformly by critics of the last four decades, including such notables as Philip Young,[11] Joseph Warren Beach,[12] Leslie Fiedler,[13] and John Aldridge, who describes her as a "compulsive bitch."[14] Almost to a person, the critics of the Brett-the-bitch school rely on Brett's own pronouncements for their interpretation, particularly the assertion that Brett makes to Jake after she leaves Romero: "You know it makes one feel rather good deciding not to be a bitch" (p. 245). This is, in fact, the single most quoted passage in criticism of the novel.

Superficially, Brett's behavior might be construed as "bitch-like." She does pursue courses of action which run counter to the wishes of the men with whom she is associated. In the early scene in the cafe, when Cohn, just introduced to Brett, fawningly asks her to dance, she lies, "I've promised to dance this with Jacob" (p. 22). Later, Jake and Brett discuss Brett's fiance, Mike Campbell, and Brett says, "Funny. I haven't thought about him for a week"; when Jake asks if she has written to Mike, Brett replies, "Not I. Never write letters" (p. 63). When Brett insists that Mike tell the story of the questionable way he received his war medals, Mike says to Cohn, "Brett will tell you. She tells all the stories that reflect discredit on me" (p. 135). Recall, in addition, Cohn's label of Circe for Brett ("she turns men into swine" p. 144) and, most important, the way Brett torments Jake by repeatedly not appearing for dates and by repeatedly describing her affairs with other men, and one can see how she, and the critics following her lead, might think of herself as a bitch.

I would strongly assert that such a charge, however, is not valid, and for three major reasons: 1. Brett and the other characters in the novel live in a milieu in which relationships and responsibilities are intentionally loose and disordered, and her behavior merely reflects this milieu; 2. While Brett's behavior toward men is sometimes thoughtless, it is never cruel; and—central to an understanding of Brett's character—3. she is a woman who, like Catherine Barkley, has a mind disordered by the impact of the war. Unlike Catherine, she cannot find the route to psychological health with the result that she consistently pursues a course of self-abuse, indeed of self-destruction.

To interpolate an historical note about the milieu: Many have recently pointed out that the twenties were not nearly so grim as Hemingway and the other expatriates portrayed them—nor, for that matter, nearly so glamorous as Scott Fitzgerald portrayed them either. For all the talk of a "lost generation," James T. Farrell claims that the years of the twenties, during which *The Sun Also Rises* is set, actually "fall within the most hopeful period of the post-Versailles world." [15] Contrary to the notion that all was either despair or glamour in the twenties, and contrary to Robert Spiller's assertion that in Hemingway "an era had found a literary voice for its skepticism and its faith," [16] historian Roderick Nash summarizes his excellent argument that the Hemingways and the Fitzgeralds were writing decidedly "minority reports" on the decade that made them both famous:

At the fringe of the American intellectual community stood a few really shaken minds for whom neither the old absolutism nor the new relativism and scientism sufficed as a basis for belief. Yet even these disillusioned few refused to exist with no values at all. Instead they began the American exploration of a point of view later labeled *existentialism*. Axiomatic to this position was confrontation with human futility and the absurdity of life. For this reason these intellectuals' conception of themselves as a lost generation was essential. Such a pose was part of a deliberate artistic experiment, an attempt not to deny value but rather to create from their own frustrated lives existential situations in which radically new values could be formulated. Despair and disillusion were dramatized in order to accentuate the achievement of confronting reality. Ernest Hemingway, F. Scott Fitzgerald, Joseph Wood Krutch, and the malcontented minority they represented were lost only by traditional standards. In their own terms they were finding new ways of defining and keeping a new faith.

As for popular thought in the 1920s, there has likewise been over-emphasis on the revolutionary and bizarre. We have read (and with the aid of records, television, and motion pictures, heard and seen) so much about the flapper, the bootlegger, and the jazz band that our conception of the era is greatly distorted. The 1920s were more than these things, just as the 1960s have been more than the jet set, hippies, and *Playboy*. We have forgotten F. Scott Fitzgerald's 1931 admonition that the jazz age concept he coined applied only to the "upper tenth of [the] nation." Perhaps even this was generous. The point is that evidence for generalizing about the mood of the decade is frequently incomplete, often by design. The twenties has been given little chance except to roar.

In fact, popular thought in these years was remarkably conservative. Beneath the eye-catching outward iconoclasm, the symbolic revolt, was a thick layer of respect for time-honored American ways, means, and rationales. The same nervousness that induced intellectuals to search for certainty prompted the general public to cling to familiar ideas with nearly hysterical intensity. It is difficult to square the popular taste of the 1920s in heroes, literature, religion, and politics, for instance, with the stereotype of the jazz age.[17]

Perhaps because of this conservatism of the twenties, many critics have been unable to empathize with the characters found in Hemingway's "minority report," and some have been quick to denounce the Hemingway milieu itself. The denunciations range from Henry S. Canby's claim that the characters of *Sun* are "lovable but futile revellers who ran from cocktail to cocktail up and down France, self-tortured, but flippant, as unmoral as monkeys,"[18] to Ernest Boyd's claim that the characters are "tragic comedians" and Hemingway himself is "a student of expatriate alcoholism,"[19] to Philip Young's charge that *Sun* is action "which goes no place,"[20] to Cleveland Chase's assertion that "it would have been difficult for Mr. Hemingway to have chosen a more dreary or aimless setting for a novel,"[21] to T. S. Matthews' comment that the action of *Sun* is "concerned with flotsam in the eddy of a backwater.''[22] Even Hemingway's mother was not to be denied a critical shot at the fictional world her son created: ''Why does he want to write about such vulgar people and such messy subjects?''[23]

The subjects are, to be sure, ''messy.'' And the characters are vulgar, though, to be fair, they are vulgar in the same ways that children and adolescents are often vulgar. They bicker about trivia as children might. In the cafe at the opening of the novel Georgette says, in response to a question from Frances Clyne, ''No, I don't like Paris. It's expensive and dirty,'' to which Frances replies, ''Really? I find it so extraordinarily clean. One of the cleanest cities in all Europe'' (p. 19). Quite childish, much like the later dialogue between Cohn and Jake about Brett, beginning with Cohn:

> ''I don't believe she would marry anybody she didn't love.''
> ''Well,'' I said. ''She's done it twice.''
> ''I don't believe it.''
> ''Well,'' I said, ''don't ask me a lot of fool questions if you don't like the answers.''
> ''I didn't ask you that.''
> ''You asked me what I knew about Brett Ashley.''
> ''I didn't ask you to insult her.''
> ''Oh, go to hell.''
> He stood up from the table his face white, and stood there white and angry behind the little plates of hors d'oeuvres.
> ''Sit down,'' I said. ''Don't be a fool.''
> ''You've got to take that back.''
> ''Oh, cut out the prep-school stuff.''
> ''Take it back.''
> ''Sure. Anything. I never heard of Brett Ashley. How's that?''
> ''No. Not that. About me going to hell.''
> ''Oh, don't go to hell,'' I said. ''Stick around. We're just starting lunch.''
> Cohn smiled again and sat down. He seemed glad to sit down. What the hell would he have done if he hadn't sat down? ''You say such damned insulting things, Jake.''
> ''I'm sorry. I've got a nasty tongue. I never mean it when I say nasty things.''

"I know it," Cohn said. "You're really about the best friend I have, Jake." [P. 39]

The most adolescent scenes of all, however, concern drinking and the high-school-like glee with which the characters describe their drunkenness. Brett urges Mike Campbell to tell the others about his experience in court, and he responds, "I don't remember. . . . I was just a little tight," to which she responds excitedly, "Tight! . . . You were blind!" (p. 136). Later, when Jake finds some of the others near the Bar Milano:

Outside the Bar Milano I found Bill and Mike and Edna. Edna was the girl's name.

"We've been thrown out," Edna said.

"By the police," said Mike. "There's some people in there that don't like me."

"I've kept them out of four fights," Edna said. "You've got to help me."

Bill's face was red.

"Come back in, Edna. There'll just be another row."

"Damned Biarritz swine," Bill said.

"Come on," Mike said. "After all, it's a pub. They can't occupy a whole pub."

"Good old Mike," Bill said. "Damned English swine come here and insult Mike and try and spoil the fiesta."

"They're so bloody," Mike said. "I hate the English."

"They can't insult Mike," Bill said. "Mike is a swell fellow. They can't insult Mike. I won't stand it. Who cares if he is a damn bankrupt?" His voice broke.

"Who cares?" Mike said. "I don't care. Jake doesn't care. Do *you* care?"

"No," Edna said. "Are you a bankrupt?"

"Of course I am. You don't care, do you, Bill?"

Bill put his arm around Mike's shoulder. [Pp. 188–89]

As the fiesta is closing, Mike and Bill find Jake in his hotel room pretending to be asleep, and Mike says approvingly, "He's blind as a tick" (p. 224).

Before judging Brett a bitch, then, one must measure both the milieu she is part of and—some of the time it means the same thing—the individuals whose interests she frustrates.

We turn now to the men with whom Brett is associated and the ways in which she denies their wishes. There is Robert Cohn, with whom she eventually agrees to have a brief affair. Cohn is, as Hemingway obviously intends him to be, the complete ass. He fawns over Brett; he follows her almost everywhere; he says all the wrong things; and he is a bully. Though Brett, in order to talk to Jake alone, says to Cohn, "For God's sake, go off somewhere. Can't you see Jake and I want to talk?" (p. 181), her outburst is probably considerably less than Cohn deserves. Far from being cruel to Cohn, on several occasions she intervenes to prevent Mike from being cruel—saying to Mike's malicious goading of Cohn, "Shut up, Michael. Try and show a little breeding" (p. 141). Because of his cruel, drunken tongue, Mike Campbell, like Cohn, deserves whatever thoughtlessness Brett directs his way.

The matter of Brett's relationship with Jake and whether she is cruel to him must be taken up in the larger context of Brett's attitude toward herself and the self-destructive behavior which grows out of that attitude. Critics have almost uniformly taken Brett's "deciding-not-to-be-a-bitch" statement at face value and accepted her assumption that she has, therefore, been a bitch all along. When critics like Edmund Wilson claim that Brett is "an exclusively destructive force," they are reinforcing Brett's interpretation of herself—and it is a wrong interpretation. Brett hurts no one in the novel nearly as severely as she hurts herself. Her nymphomania, her alcoholism, her constant fits of depression, and her obsession with bathing are all symptoms of an individual engaged in a consistent pattern of self-abuse. Even in causing discomfort to Jake—much of which he sets himself up for—Brett causes even greater discomfort to herself. Before one too easily accepts Robert Cohn's view of Brett as the emasculating Circe, as critic Sheridan Baker and others do,[24] one must realize that Jake was not technically emasculated (as Hemingway made clear),[25] and that the injury the war (a male-mission enterprise) caused Jake is far more permanent and devastating than anything that Brett does to him.

The most significant symptom of Brett's pursuit of self-destruction is her nymphomania. Two of the basic interpretations of nymphomania are 1. that it is merely the open expression of the "natural" female sexual appetite of insatiation which, because of centuries of social restrictions (produced by male sexual limitations), is suppressed in most women;[26] and 2.—the more commonly held of the two—that it represents a woman's attempt to overcome social or sexual self-doubt, by demonstrating, through one sexual experience after another, that she is, in fact, attractive, desirable, wanted.[27] By the first interpretation, Brett's milieu could be said to allow freedom from most conventions, including those of female sexual suppression, but I am convinced it is the second of the interpretations of nymphomania which more aptly applies in Brett's case. Her unsuccessful marriages, her engagement to a man she has no serious regard for, her inability to commit herself to anything meaningful—indeed her inability even to define what is meaningful—denote a mental confusion in Brett, on the matter of her own worth, which is compounded by her chronic cycle of drinking-drunkenness-recovery. Another, overlapping, cycle taints Brett's mind as well: alcohol-sex-guilt. Despite the ostensible isolation of Brett and her group from the mores of the world at large, not even Brett can completely dismiss the attitudes (in this case, regarding female drinking and sexuality) of the prevailing culture which surrounds a subculture group.

Brett's mind is, then, seriously disordered and filled with guilt. But how does this condition reflect on Brett's relationship with Jake? Quite directly actually. As psychiatrist Eric Berne points out, guilty people feel a compulsion to provide themselves with punishment; they almost always "set the stage" of their lives so as to insure themselves of painful events, thus constantly providing themselves with the punishment that their mental states require.[28] Jake's physical condition provides precisely the kind of constant pain which Brett needs. When critics like Sheldon Grebstein claim that Brett is the "most dramatic example . . . of how pure sex can waste lives,"[29] they overlook the rather obvious fact that Brett's sexual activity reflects not her threshold of lust but rather her threshold of self-abasement. Jake is the

58   CASSANDRA'S DAUGHTERS

perfect vehicle. She can (with his encouragement) sexually tease
him and herself. Midway through the arousal stage, she can step
back melodramatically, acknowledge the impossibility of it all,
and torment herself for initiating the action in the first place.

Such scenes of torment between Jake and Brett are common
in the novel and much of the time they have the mock-serious-
ness of the soap opera. Near the opening, in the taxi, they kiss;
then "she turned away and pressed against the corner of the seat,
as far away as she could get." She says, "Don't touch me. . . .
Please don't touch me" (p. 25). Later in the hotel, Jake asks,
"Couldn't we just live together?" and Brett replies, "I'd just
tromper you with everybody. You couldn't stand it" (p. 55).
Still later in the cafe Brett tells Jake: "I'm so miserable," and
then goes on to insure herself of a continued feeling of misery
by telling Jake, "Good night, darling. I won't see you again"
(pp. 64–65). Even the book's conclusion reflects the tease-with-
draw-suffer syndrome that has become a routine part of Brett's
relationship with Jake. In a tone of agony befitting television
"daytime drama," Brett says, "Oh, Jake . . . we could have
had such a damned good time together" (p. 247).

In Brett's relationship with Romero, we see two aspects of
Brett's character that demonstrate that she is a self-induced
"sufferer" but that she is *not* a bitch. Early on she reminds herself, "That Romero lad is just a child" (p. 167), but adds, "And
God, what looks" (p. 168). She ups the ante on her guilt not
long afterward when she tells Jake (guilt coming from both di-
rections this way), "I'm a goner. I'm mad about the Romero
boy. I'm in love with him, I think," and follows immediately
with the guilt pay-off when she says, "I've never felt such a
bitch" (p. 184). Brett is better than she wants to think herself,
however, for this time she would not be causing discomfort to
someone who deserves it (like Cohn and Mike Campbell) or to
someone who consistently asks for it (like Jake). To hurt Romero would be a bitch-like act and she cannot do it. Despite what
she thinks, it is simply not her style. Brett is confused; she feels
guilty (hence the obsession with bathing);[30] she is tragically self-
destructive; but in no legitimate way can she be interpreted as a
bitch.

MARGOT MACOMBER

It is paradoxical that the Hemingway short story that has received the most critical attention—"The Short Happy Life of Francis Macomber"—is also the one which for forty years has been the most flagrantly misread. "Macomber" is among the list of seven or so Hemingway stories consistently selected as the author's most outstanding.[31] Its heroine, Margot Macomber, is, however, not only the most critically maligned female character since Lady Macbeth but also the most serious victim of inaccurate "party-line" criticism in all of Hemingway. Like the Brett-Ashley-the-bitch line of criticism, the school which labels Margot Macomber not only a bitch but a murderess as well appears to have begun with Edmund Wilson. During the forty years since Wilson's pronouncements on Margot, dozens of critics have followed his line of misinterpretation, while only a handful— notably Warren Beck,[32] Virgil Hutton,[33] and Robert B. Holland[34]—have accepted the words of Hemingway's objective narrator to mean exactly what they say.

Holland presents a very useful summary of the critics who have followed Edmund Wilson's lead in charging Margot Macomber with the murder of her husband. He lists, and quotes from, Ray B. West, Jr., Philip Young, Carlos Baker, John Killinger, Leslie Fiedler, Joseph DeFalco, André Maurois, Theodore Bardacke, William Bysshe Stein, and Arthur Waterman.[35] Holland could have added many other critics to the list, including Pier Francesco Paolini, who claims: "Macomber's wife Margot, with the fierce primal instincts of a she-wolf leading the pack, reviles her husband for his weakness. . . . Then, when Macomber redeems himself and, in a happy moment, a fatal moment, feels he is beginning a new life . . . she cold-bloodedly shoots him."[36] Or Oliver Evans: "This conception of women, that they can live comfortably with their men only when the latter are dead morally, may be found also in that other, simpler story about Africa that Hemingway wrote about the same time, 'The Short Happy Life of Francis Macomber,' where Margot, when her husband belatedly asserts his identity, shoots him."[37]

One of the most unfortunate aspects of this particular party-line of criticism—other than its being flatly wrong—is that it continues to perpetuate itself. Even during the last ten or fifteen years there has been a veritable spate of Ph.D. dissertations following the same shopworn line on Margot Macomber. From Naomi Grant: "But Margot sees her own death in Macomber's newborn courage. She cannot recover the ascendancy she has lost. . . . Margot can seem to aim words at one objective and make them hit another. She strikes out at Macomber, while seeming to attack Wilson. She handles the Mannlicher with the same deadly precison."[38] From Lemuel Byrd: "Margot finally murders Francis."[39] From Sharon Dean: "Representative of the full-fledged bitch is Margot Macomber, though to give Hemingway credit she becomes a bitch only after trying to make a successful marriage with a cowardly husband. Margot finally so needs to dominate the husband she despises that she kills him when he becomes a man she might have loved."[40] And from Mimi Gladstein: "Once Francis has shown his courage and by extension his manhood, she extracts the ultimate sacrifice, his life."[41]

Implicit in these observations, as in most other critical assertions about "Macomber," are two additional party-line notions about the story: 1. that Margot is a bitch; and 2. that Francis is on a safari quest for his "manhood," and that, having "found" it, he must be destroyed. All three of these assumptions are, interestingly enough, merely echoes of the perception of the guide Robert Wilson. Most critics have unfortunately accepted Wilson's perceptions as valid and have adopted them themselves. Some, like Naomi Grant, do so because they view Wilson as Hemingway's "code hero."[42] A few even carry the notion of Wilson's credibility to extreme lengths, critics such as Pier Paolini, who claims strangely that Wilson "is in his own way a genuine humanitarian."[43]

Warren Beck[44] spends considerable effort illustrating that Robert Wilson's perception of people and events is not to be trusted—an effort so thorough that it leaves me little to do except to summarize Wilson's moral deficiencies (which obviously impair his ability to judge circumstances clearly). Wilson is, first of all, cruel: he whips his native gun-bearers and camp helpers even though such acts are illegal, let alone inhumane (p. 6).[45] He is insensitive: when he does not enjoy talking with Macomber anymore, he simply insults him (p. 7). He is an adulterer: he quickly takes Margot to bed when the opportunity presents itself and the commentary about his double cot suggests that it is one of his regular safari services (p. 23). He is, in effect, a moral whore: when thinking about what he, as white hunter, is expected to do for his clients, we are told, "their standards were his standards as long as they were hiring him" (p. 26). He is a bully: at the close of the story, he verbally pounds Margot into submission— immediately after her husband's death—then gloats to her, "Please is much better. Now I'll stop" (p. 37). Worst of all— in addition to the implications of the narrative description of Wilson as having "flat, blue, machine-gunner's eyes" (p. 8), and the probably accurate, though tactless, observation from Margot that Wilson would "kill anything" (p. 8)—Wilson quite willingly becomes an accessory-after-the-fact in what he clearly views as a murder case.

Notwithstanding all the reasons not to accept Robert Wilson's vision of life or of events in the story as valid, nearly every critic treating the story has not only accepted Wilson's standards, as Francis Macomber does, but has used those standards himself in interpreting the behavior of the Macombers. On the issue of Francis "coming to manhood," Francis himself, following Wilson's lead and embarrassed by having run from the lion, feels compelled to "reclaim" himself: "Maybe I can fix it up on buffalo" (p. 8) and later, "I'd like to clear away that lion business" (p. 11). Following his shooting of the buffalo, the act which, according to conventional wisdom, insures Francis' "manhood," he says, "You know something did happen to me. . . . I feel absolutely different" (p. 32)—a reflection of the sentiment that is passing through Wilson's mind at the same time: "It's that some of them stay little boys so long, Wilson thought. . . . The great American boy-men. Damned strange people. But he liked this Macomber now. . . . He'd seen it in the war work the same way. More of a change than any loss of virginity. Fear gone like an operation. Something else grew in its place. Main thing a man had. Made him into a man'' (p. 33).

Beginning with Edmund Wilson, the critics quickly adopted most of the hunter-Wilson's ethic. Edmund Wilson says that Francis "saves his soul at the last minute." [46] Eight years later, Ray B. West, Jr., would claim oddly that Francis' act went even beyond "manhood" to become "man's final victory over death." [47] Seven years after that Pier Paolini would claim that Francis "lives long enough to feel his veins pulsate with the rhythm of genuine living" [48]—a position that would be given an existential flavor in four more years by John Killinger, who says that Francis' act is "his awakening, his beginning to ex-ist." [49] During the sixties Joseph DeFalco would say, "The victory of Macomber over himself releases him," [50] and Philip Young would say, "It is these shooting standards which Macomber eventually learns and which, although they bring his death, make him for a short happy lifetime a man." [51] Among numerous others of the seventies, Pamella Farley says that Francis "comes of age when suddenly precipitated into action." [52]

Having found Wilson's perception of the events of the story lacking, let us examine the ethic he believes in, which Francis and the critics have so eagerly embraced—that to be a "man," one must demonstrate a knowledge of the protocol of the big-game-hunting-safari (recall Wilson's admonitions about how much money to give the natives, about how inappropriate it is to ask a guide not to reveal one's hunting failures, and about how one "must" follow a wounded animal and destroy it); he must demonstrate precision in firing a high-caliber hunting rifle (remember Wilson's disgust at Francis for "gut-shooting" the lion); he must demonstrate a willingness to stand in the face of a charging lion or buffalo regardless of how likely it is that he, or his guide, can stop the animal by shooting it; and he must be able to "control" his woman.

Putting aside for the moment the ability of Francis Macomber to meet these requirements for "manhood," it seems to me that the requirements themselves are patently silly. Hemingway, in part, knew that, and his critics certainly should have. How strange a notion to think that shooting at a large, often stupid, animal at some distance with a cannon-powered rifle—or worse, to poise oneself unflinchingly in front of a crazed beast—somehow constitutes a sensible (even decent) test of what is called human courage, much less, as Edmund Wilson claims, saves one's "soul," or worse, as Ray West, Jr., claims, insures one a "final victory over death." What a melodramatic and adolescent notion of worthwhile human endeavor! If, as Philip Young suggests, Francis "completely disgraces himself"[53] by not meeting Wilson's criteria for "manhood," could one not be said to be equally "disgraced" by failing, on the first attempt, to execute a nearly perfect dive from the Acapulco cliffs; by failing, on first attempt, to lean forward over the horns of an enraged and charging bull and plunge the sword into the precise spot at the back of the head which will kill it; by failing, on first attempt, to keep up with a party of seasoned climbers as they ascend the sheer face of a mountain? In his unpublished and untitled "African Journal," Hemingway says, "I had realized long before why white hunters were paid as well as they were and I understood why they shifted camp to hunt their clients where they could protect them accurately"[54]—the assumption here that guides simply protect their clients, nothing at all about expecting male clients to "come to manhood."

Francis Macomber, despite his deficiencies, does have abilities: "He knew about . . . motorcycles—that was earliest—about motor cars, about duck-shooting, about fishing, trout, salmon and big-sea, about sex in books, many books, too many books, about all court games, about dogs, not much about horses, about hanging on to his money, about most of the other things his world dealt in, and about his wife not leaving him" (p. 21). In addition to which (and certainly considered a measurement of success in most cultures), "he was very wealthy, and would be much wealthier" (p. 21). How ridiculous, then, to pull a near-middle-age businessman from the milieu which he understands and in which he has proven himself a substantial success, transplant him in a milieu 7,000 miles away which is utterly alien to him, expect a level of performance from him which is nearly equal to that of the professional whose life has been spent there, and, when his performance falls short, blithely claim that he has flunked his test of "manhood."

Even the validity of the big-game hunting enterprise itself, it seems to me—as it does to Margot Macomber—is open to serious question. There is something not particularly admirable, despite all the protocol and mock-heroism, about the destruction of such animals simply to provide income for the guide and to provide a manufactured self-concept of "courage" for the one paying the guide. There is nothing admirable about Wilson telling Macomber to shoot the lion "in the neck if you can make it. Shoot for bone. Break him down" (p. 12); or Wilson telling Macomber, after the lion has been wounded, "Let him get sick before we follow him up" (p. 16) and "We'll let him stiffen up a bit and then you and I'll go in and have a look for him" (p. 17); or Wilson saying excitedly, when Macomber shoots the buffalo, "That does it. . . . Got the spine" (p. 29).

This brings us to another misinterpretation of the story—that Margot's early unpleasant behavior is largely the result of her husband's cowardice and the consequent shame and embarrassment she feels. Such an interpretation is based on what I consider the inaccurate assumption that, like Francis (and subsequently most critics), Margot endorses Robert Wilson's standards of "courage" and "manhood." Far more troubling to her, it seems to me, is 1. the hunting enterprise itself; and 2. the hypocrisy of the two men as they conspire to make the enterprise a philosophical statement of courage *writ large* in Francis' life. Her perception of the hunting enterprise, though sarcastically rendered, is accurate: "You were lovely this morning. That is if blowing things' heads off is lovely" (p. 9). Later, when Francis says that he must kill the second lion, Margot says, "Well, that's what you're out here for, isn't it?" (p. 13).

It is the hypocrisy of the whole affair which most galls Margot. Near the beginning, despite the fact that Francis has run from the lion and Wilson has had to kill it, Wilson, back at camp, says to Francis, "You've got your lion . . . and a damned fine one too," following which, we are told, "Mrs. Macomber looked at Wilson quickly" (p. 4). Margot resents the charade that the two are involved in on behalf of Macomber's "quest for courage." Shortly afterward, when Francis mentions the matter of the lion, Wilson dishonestly says, "Forget the whole thing. Nothing to it anyway" (p. 6). As the ante on Francis' quest is raised by two more "failures" (his gut-shooting the second lion, then running from it), Margot realizes how intensely the two men have drawn together in a conspiracy to manufacture some courage for Francis. When they learn that the buffalo is not dead after all and must be pursued, Margot says, "Then it's going to be just like the lion" (p. 30), to which Wilson, now Macomber's committed advocate, heatedly replies, "It's not going to be a damned bit like the lion" (p. 31).

Margot's kissing Wilson in the car and her later bout in bed with him are not efforts to punish Francis for his cowardice, but attempts to break up the conspiracy of male hypocrisy in which the two men are so earnestly engaged. These two acts and much that she says could well be used as evidence that Margot can be an unpleasant person at times (on occasion bitch-like, if one insists). She is cerainly sarcastic: "How is the beautiful red-faced Mr. Wilson? Are you feeling better, Francis, my pearl?" (p. 8); to Francis' "You think that I'll take anything" (after her sexual episode with Wilson), "I know you will, sweet" (p. 23); "If you make a scene I'll leave you, darling" (p. 25); "Just because you've chased some helpless animals in a motor car you talk like heroes" (p. 33). Add to these comments Francis' observation, "You *are* a bitch" (p. 22) and Robert Wilson's series of observations: "They [American women] are . . . the hardest, the cruelest, the most predatory and the most attractive" (p. 8); "She is away for twenty minutes and now she is back, simply enamelled in that American female cruelty" (p. 9); "They govern, of course, and to govern one has to be cruel sometimes. Still, I've seen enough of their damn terrorism" (p. 10) and the picture that emerges is not a wholesome one, particularly as Hemingway is known to have said about Margot, "I invented her . . . from the worst bitch I knew."[55]

My purpose here is not to prove that Margot is *not* a bitch, but to point out that, compared with Robert Wilson and her husband, who are her chief judges, she is not all that bad, and she is decidedly *not* a murderess. I have already treated Wilson's moral frailties. I would note about Francis Macomber that Margot is quite right in despising him as a "weak" individual, but he is weak, as she sees, not because he runs from lions, but because he so eagerly encourages others (in this case, Robert Wilson) to set the standards by which he measures his own worth, instead of setting them himself. In keeping with this interpretation, Francis remains weak to the end of the story. By standing firm in front of the charging buffalo, he confirms his sense of self-worth according to Wilson's standards, but he dies continuing to "prove" himself by a standard not his own.

The nearly unanimous interpretation of Margot Macomber as murderess (the logical extension of Robert Wilson's manhood-bitch thesis) is established by Wilson's cocksure comments, "That was a pretty thing to do. . . . He *would* have left you too" and "Why didn't you poison him? That's what they do in England" (pp. 36–37). This is patently wrong. It reflects more than anything else the manner in which the guide would deal with troublesome matters—the low threshold for firearm solutions which leads him earlier, as he rides in the car with the Macombers the day after his sexual experience with Margot, to fear that Francis might "take a notion to blow the back of my head off" (p. 25). The murder thesis is wrong for three reasons: 1. it looks as though the charging buffalo will kill Francis in another two seconds anyway, making his murder superfluous and unnecessarily dangerous legally; 2. there is insufficient time for Margot to see that the buffalo was not dead and was charging, to size up the opportunity, and to carry out the technical acts of preparing and firing the Mannlicher; and, most important, 3. the text of the story says otherwise. In support of these three arguments, I suggest an examination of the passage relating the buffalo charge and the shooting:

"He's dead in there," Wilson said. "Good work," and he turned to grip Macomber's hand and as they shook hands, grinning at each other, the gun-bearer shouted wildly and they saw him coming out of the bush sideways, fast as a crab, and the bull coming, nose out, mouth tight closed, blood dripping, massive head straight out, coming in a charge, his little pig eyes bloodshot as he looked at them. Wilson, who was ahead was kneeling shooting, and Macomber, as he fired, unhearing his shot in the roaring of Wilson's gun, saw fragments like slate burst from the huge boss of the horns, and the head jerked, he shot again at the wide nostrils and saw the horns jolt again and fragments fly, and he did not see Wilson now and, aiming carefully, shot again with the buffalo's huge bulk almost on him and his rifle almost level with the on-coming head, nose out, and he could see the little wicked eyes and the head started to lower and he felt a sudden white-hot, blinding flash explode inside his head and that was all he ever felt.

Wilson had ducked to one side to get in a shoulder shot. Macomber had stood solid and shot for the nose, shooting a touch high each time and hitting the heavy horns, splintering and chipping them like hitting a slate roof, and Mrs. Macomber, in the car, had shot at the buffalo with the 6.5 Mannlicher as it seemed about to gore Macomber and had hit her husband about two inches up and a little to one side of the base of his skull.

Francis Macomber lay now, face down, not two yards from where the buffalo lay on his side and his wife knelt over him with Wilson beside her. [Pp. 35–36]

The first argument is self-evident. The "buffalo's huge bulk [was] almost on" Macomber, "the head started to lower" for the impact, and Macomber ends "face down, not two yards from where the buffalo lay." The second argument requires a bit more explanation. Given Macomber's moderate level of familiarity with the Springfield .30-06 rifle he is holding, and given the probability that the rifle is chamber-loaded, with the safety on, at the moment of the buffalo's sudden charge, it is highly unlikely that Macomber's three shots (including the two necessary movements of the bolt) would require more than four seconds. That means that Margot Macomber, being farther away, would probably not have seen the buffalo charge out of the brush until a moment after Francis sees him (thereby losing at least part of a second). She has slightly more than three seconds, then, to see the buffalo, note that Francis is standing directly between the buffalo and herself, realize that such a position could make the murder of her husband appear to be an accident, pick up the Mannlicher (not a single word indicates that she has any familiarity with it or that she has ever fired a gun in her life), move the bolt to chamber-load the rifle (assuming that Wilson has left the rifle magazine-loaded in the car, something a professional hunter would be unlikely to do), aim the rifle at her husband's moving head, and fire. In three seconds? Simply impossible.

The final argument against Margot's being a murderess is found in the text itself. Hemingway's narrator, who has shown impeccable reliability throughout the story, says flatly, "Mrs. Macomber, in the car, had shot *at the buffalo* with the 6.5 Mannlicher . . . [my emphasis]" (p. 36). *Not* "at Francis, while pretending to shoot at the buffalo," *or* " 'accidentally' shot her husband" (the unfathomable extrapolation of a number of critics)—but plain and simply "had shot at the buffalo." Given the abundant evidence that two generations of critics have read those words and, by choosing to accept as accurate Robert Wilson's perceptions of Macomber's "manhood," Margot's "bitchhood," and the killing itself, have chosen not to believe them, one is forced to accept Robert Holland's judgment that "to an author like Hemingway, to whom the integrity of the word was a religion, the critical fate of 'The Short Happy Life of Francis Macomber' must have been, if he knew of it, a sad example of scholarly ineptitude at best and of irresponsible thesis-hunting at worst. It should indeed be a cause of profound wonder to us all that well-educated scholars can write, and reputable journals publish, material whose first premise is based on plain failure to read literally what is, literally, on the page." [56]

HELEN

The most undeserving victim of the party-line criticism on Hemingway's "bitch-women" is Helen, in "The Snows of Kilimanjaro." Once again, the progenitor of the line of criticism which labels Helen a bitch (and the corrupter and destroyer of an artist's talent as well) is Edmund Wilson. The surprising uniformity of negative criticism about Helen may partly be due to the close proximity in time during which "Macomber" and "Snows" were published, and, since both are set in Africa, the two works have been viewed, for the most part, as "companion" stories. Several of the major assumptions made about "Macomber" are thought automatically to apply as well to "Snows." Whatever else may lie behind the critical notions about the two stories, the most undeserving victim is Helen, who is tainted by the spillover of "bitch" assertions made about Margot Macomber. Edmund Wilson started it off by saying, "The men in both these African stories are married to American bitches of the most soul-destroying sort."[57] (Robert W. Lewis, Jr.,[58] incidentally, raises the intriguing, though minor, question of whether or not Harry and Helen are, in fact, married. The story gives no clue beyond Harry saying to Helen, "if you hadn't left your own people . . . *to take me on*—"[p. 55],[59] and later the narrator saying, "she *had acquired him*" [p. 62]—my emphasis.)

A decade later Carlos Baker would echo Edmund Wilson on the relationships between the stories and between the women: "the focal point in each is the corrupting power of women and money, two of the forces aggressively mentioned in *The Green Hills of Africa* as impediments to American writing men"[60]— an echo that makes its way into the recent work of Leon Linderoth, who says "both stories deal with the corrupting forces of women and money."[61] Add to these assertions such refinements as Philip Young's "There is no question that the protagonist Harry is the Hemingway hero";[62] Leslie Fiedler's interpretation that Helen "with her wealth has weaned her husband from all that sustained his virility, betrayed him to aimlessness and humiliation";[63] Naomi Grant's "So Helen leads her husband from the Eden of accomplishment into the exile of frustrated escape";[64] and Oliver Evans' brutal comments, "Of the various death symbols, Helen is the most important," and "she thrives, as would the hyena, on *what is dead in him*"[65]—and we have the devastating conventional-wisdom portrait of Helen. She is, in Harry's own words, a "rich bitch" (p. 60), and, so the interpretation goes, the financial security and comfort which she represents have ruined the promising career of a gifted American writer.

Ridiculous. Despite the time and geographical proximity of "Macomber" and "Snows" (and the resultant proximity, in many critics' minds, of Margot Macomber and Helen), despite the critical line of such luminaries as Wilson, Young, Baker, and Fiedler, despite the fact that Helen may have been modeled unfavorably on Hemingway's second wife, Pauline[66]—indeed, despite *Green Hills of Africa*—what is *in* the story is this: a man, Harry, who is (and for a long time has been) weak, cowardly, dishonest, and cruel; and a woman who is strong, considerate, and deeply loving.

Examples of weaknesses in Harry's character are legion throughout the story. The professional impotence which he has experienced for some time manifests itself, by the time of the action of the story, in a barrage of self-pitying, cowardly, and cruel observations. The bitterness of these perceptions is compounded by the fact that he is now literally dying, whereas before he was merely partly dead morally. At the beginning of the story, and briefly a few times later, he shows minimal consideration for Helen ("I'm awfully sorry about the odor," p. 52), but his manner of behavior is almost entirely abusive. Even when he says, "I don't want to hurt you," he follows immediately with: "All right then. I'll go on hurting you. It's more amusing. The only thing I ever really liked to do with you I can't do now" (p. 58). To Helen's plaintive question about whether it is necessary for him to destroy everything as he dies ("I mean do you have to take away everything? Do you have to kill your horse, and your wife and burn your saddle and your armour?"), Harry answers selfishly, "I don't like to leave anything" (p. 58).

It is very difficult to account for the reading which Edmund Wilson and others give "Snows of Kilimanjaro." Wilson says of the relationship between Harry and Helen that Helen "has debased him."[67] The assumption is that Harry came to his association with Helen morally whole and professionally active, and neither is the case. Furthermore, the relationship between

Helen's wealth and Harry's decline is never established. Proximity is once again a factor, no doubt, in the widespread misinterpretations of the story; Helen is simply close at hand when Harry's long string finally runs out, so the blame falls on her. The myth of Harry as "corrupted" writer is one that even Harry can sustain only part of the time. Early in the story, with reference to his coming death, he thinks, "Now he would never write the things that he had saved to write until he knew enough to write them well" (p. 54)—a self-serving interpretation of the recent unproductive years of his life. In fact, Harry dried up years before, long before he met Helen. In his honest moments he admits it: "It was not her fault that when he went to her he was already over" (p. 59); "He had destroyed his talent by not using it, by betrayals of himself and what he believed in, by drinking so much that he blunted the edge of his perceptions, by laziness, by sloth, and by snobbery" (p. 60). Harry has already answered the question that he asks later, when thinking about his ranch experiences: "He knew at least twenty good stories from out there and he had never written one. Why?" (p. 72).

Like most writers, Harry is a man of considerable ego. How, then, does he confront the very evident fact that for a long period of time he has produced practically nothing? (Though Helen at one time regarded him as a writer of some reputation, there is nothing to suggest that he was ever the "gifted" artist that many critics have assumed him to be as they build their case against Helen.) Apparently much earlier in his career, Harry concluded that there was more risk of failure in continuing to write than in seeking comfortable situations with a series of increasingly rich women. "What was his talent anyway? It was a talent all right but instead of using it, he had traded on it. . . . It was strange, too, wasn't it, that when he fell in love with another woman, that woman should always have more money than the last one?" (p. 60); and "He had sold vitality, in one form or another, all his life and when your affections are not involved you give much better value for the money" (p. 61).

Harry has been both a parasite and a whore for years. Like a whore, his affection, if not his sexual gratification, is fake. After he tells Helen that he loves her, we are told: "He slipped into the familiar lie he made his bread and butter by" (p. 58); later: "How could a woman know that you meant nothing that you said; that you spoke only from habit and to be comfortable? After he no longer meant what he said, his lies were more successful with women than when he had told them the truth" (p. 59). In his self-deluding periods Harry can have it both ways. He can have the luxury and security of the opulent life; he can, at the same time, free himself from having to write (and the fear that he will not be able to) by citing the "corrupting" influence of his rich women. He plays this game with Helen—as he no doubt played it with his earlier women—with random accusing comments: "Your bloody money" (p. 54); "Your damned money was my armour" (p. 58); "this rich bitch, this kindly caretaker and destroyer of his talent" (p. 60). These comments are probably responsible for Helen's consignment to the "Hemingway-bitch" category, an assessment paralleling the one in "Macomber" in which critics have accepted as valid Robert Wilson's judgments about Francis' manhood, Margot's bitchhood, and the "murder" of Francis. In the case of the critics adopting Harry's designation of Helen as a bitch, it is even less excusable; unlike the consistently cynical Wilson, Harry wavers in his belittling interpretation of Helen, using the "rich bitch" designation only in his more dishonest and self-serving moments.

At other times his perceptions, particularly involving himself and Helen, become clear. He acknowledges his own responsibility for his failure as a writer, as well as Helen's steadfast performance as a thoughtful and loving companion. As the two have a drink after Helen shoots the Tommy ram, Harry thinks: "She *was* good to him. He had been cruel and unjust in the afternoon. She was a fine woman, marvellous really" (p. 64). Later, in what appears to be an uncharacteristically honest comment, he tells Helen, "You're a fine woman" (p. 67). Such observations suggest that Harry, on occasion, knows better than to charge Helen with his failure, though the critics may not.

And well he should. Helen, as portrayed in the story, is an exceptional individual. She gives where Harry takes. She is magnanimous where Harry is petty. She is thoughtful where Harry is both thoughtless and cruel. It is little short of amazing that Helen is so glibly labeled a bitch, a destroyer, even death itself, when there is not a single instance in the story of her being unpleasant in any way. She shows unwavering concern for Harry and the story gives every evidence that she has always shown it. She continually asks what she can do to make him comfortable. In response to his accusations, she gently reminds him: "I left everything and I went wherever you wanted to go and I've done what you wanted to do" (p. 55); "I'll always love you" (p. 55); "You liked to do many things and everything you wanted to do I did" (p. 58). Her automatic thoughtfulness is evidenced when she goes some distance to hunt the Tommy ram so she would not disturb the animals near the camp that Harry enjoys watching ("She was always thoughtful, he thought"—p. 59) and again when she decides to join him in a drink, though she knows drinking is harmful to him, rather than nag him about his drinking and force him to drink alone.

Helen, in fact, possesses virtually every characteristic that Harry—and probably most men—finds attractive in women. In addition to the thoughtfulness already discussed, she is intelligent and articulate, and reference to the "book bag" suggests that she is well-read. She evidently genuinely loves Harry and admires him for what he at least once was ("She liked what he wrote," p. 61). She avoids nagging Harry, as in the matter of the drinking, and is, as Harry describes her, "still a good-looking woman . . . and she had a pleasant body. She had a great talent and appreciation for the bed" (p. 61). Harry comments several times on Helen's sexuality—as on the fact that "she shot very well" (p. 60). Helen, it seems, is not only physically sexual: "She looked at him with her well-known, well-loved face from *Spur* and *Town and Country*, only a little the worse for drink, only a little the worse for bed, but *Town and Country* never showed those good breasts and those useful thighs and those lightly small-of-back caressing hands" (p. 67)—she is verbally sexual as well. When Harry says, "I'd like to destroy you a few times in bed," she replies, "Yes. That's the good destruction.

That's the way we're made to be destroyed" (p. 63), and near the end: "You're the most complete man I've ever known" (p. 74).

In marked contrast to Harry, Helen is exceptionally strong. She has experienced a series of tragedies: "Her husband had died when she was still a comparatively young woman and for a while she had devoted herself to her two just-grown children, who did not need her and were embarrassed at having her about"; "Then one of her two children was killed in a plane crash" (p. 61); and now Harry is dying. But unlike Harry, who is the symbol of moral and physical death, whose philosophy of cowardice is succinctly captured by his thought, "no thing could hurt him if he did not care" (p. 72), Helen amply demonstrates the moral substance to build a satisfactory new life out of the wreckage of the old one, despite the misinterpretations of her character by the critics.

DOROTHY BRIDGES

Not nearly so widely treated in criticism as Brett Ashley, Margot Macomber, or Helen is Dorothy Bridges from Hemingway's only full-length play, *The Fifth Column*.[68] There is relatively little detailed criticism on the play at all. Assessments of Dorothy, however (as well as the play), are, like those of Brett, Margot, and Helen, almost uniformly negative. Of those making unflattering observations on the play, there are Lionel Trilling, who, in speaking favorably of *For Whom the Bell Tolls*, says of Hemingway, "He does not, as in the period of *To Have and Have Not* and *The Fifth Column*, warp or impede his notable talent with the belief that art is to be used like the automatic rifle";[69] Philip Young, who describes *The Fifth Column* as "a play full of wonderful talk but Rover boy action";[70] Allen Guttmann, who calls it "a wooden play [which makes] clear that Hemingway could not dramatize the Spanish war with these stick figures; the play violates its author's own often-repeated rule—the writer must always tell the truth as he sees it";[71] Maxwell Geismar, who speaks of "the facile enthusiasm of [Hemingway's] political play";[72] Carlos Baker who observes that Hemingway later told "anyone who would listen that he ought to have written *The Fifth Column* as a novel";[73] and Leo Gurko who takes a mild slap at both Hemingway and the play: "Ernest Hemingway came to Spain on assignment as a reporter; he left with plans for a play, *The Fifth Column*, and a novel, *For Whom the Bell Tolls*. The civil war might have been made to order for him; it embodied most of the salient features of the script Hemingway had been working with for fifteen years: two sides fighting with unbridled ferocity, every known variety of cowardice and heroism, characters who were *aficionado* and characters who were not, and a backdrop of great events against which the fortunes of selected individuals could be projected in dimensions somewhat larger than life."[74]

The word on Dorothy has been no better: John Killinger categorizes Dorothy as one of Hemingway's "bad" women, one of those who "are demanding, who constrict the liberty of the heroes, who attempt to possess them";[75] Theodore Bardacke calls Dorothy "a vain, empty and useless daughter of the American middle class";[76] Philip Young says that Dorothy "is rich, she is unconscious of the class meaning of the war, and she takes time from [Philip's] work";[77] Lemuel Byrd says that Dorothy "has about the same effect on Philip Rawlings that Brett Ashley has on Jake Barnes: she is an emotional strain on the male";[78] Pamella Farley says that Dorothy "plagues [Philip] more than the fascists";[79] and Leon Linderoth places Dorothy in that category of Hemingway females "who, though they do not actively corrupt a man, nonetheless cramp his style. These girls could well develop into true bitches of the Macomber type."[80]

Before we take at face value the unflattering commentary on Dorothy, we should first—as we must with Brett Ashley—examine the milieu in which the action occurs and the male characters with whom Dorothy is associated and by whom, in large part, she is judged. Unlike *The Sun Also Rises*, set in the residue of war, *The Fifth Column* concerns war itself—the intermittent Fascist shelling in the vicinity of Madrid's Hotel Florida, where most of the play takes place, espionage, counterespionage, murder, and torture—to say nothing of chronic drunkenness, whoring, and overlapping sexual affairs. Hardly the climate to bring out one's most notable attributes.

More important than the war to Dorothy, however, is the influence of the men with whom she has relationships, first, Preston but particularly Philip Rawlings. Preston appears, from the little we see of him, to be a Robert Cohn figure (without boxing talent). He is the first to "go below" when the shelling starts. Dorothy claims that he cheaply uses stories of his wife and children "as sort of an opening wedge to get into bed with some one" (p. 25); after Philip pummels him and he is thrown out of his room (just before he disappears from the play altogether), the most that Preston can manage by way of reprisal is his parting whine, "You're a rotten cad, Rawlings. Remember I told you, will you?" (p. 29).

It is Philip, though, with whom Dorothy is in love, who has the greatest impact on her life and who is most unfair to her. Philip plays the same double game with Dorothy he plays for the general public. His "cover" is that of a journalist who is drunken and degenerate in most ways and who rarely makes any effort to do his work; in fact, he is a fanatically dedicated Communist counterespionage agent whose job is to ferret out, capture, and sometimes kill the "fifth-column" Fascists who live among and regularly assassinate the citizens of Madrid. The problem with this dual-appearance arrangement, where Dorothy is concerned, is that she knows only one side—the Philip Rawlings who, like a character from *The Sun Also Rises*, picks up a cuspidor at the bar, Chicote's, and goes "around blessing people out of it. You know, sprinkling it on them" (p. 5), and who takes adolescent delight in not remembering his drunken revels of the night before: "Mention something and see if I recall it" (p. 14); who enters the room rudely saying, "Salud, Comrade Bastard Preston. Salud Comrade Boredom Bridges" (p. 7); who patronizingly says to the Spanish electrician, "Come in, Comrade Marconi" and of the Moorish whore, Anita, "And here's a Moorish comrade. . . . She's awfully shy" (p. 7); who enjoys beating the harmless Preston and later bullying him out of his room; who enjoys being frivolous: "Lovely place, Gibraltar. I had a most unusual experience there once" (p. 8); and who enjoys teasing Dorothy with aimless chatter:

Philip. I'll be back in a moment, darling. And I'll be *so* serious.

Dorothy. You know what you said?

Philip. Of course.

Dorothy. [*Very happily*] You said *Darling*.

Philip. I knew it was infectious but I never knew it was contagious. Forgive me, *dear*.

Dorothy. Dear is a nice word, too.

Philip. Good-bye then—er—sweet.

Dorothy. Sweet, oh you *darling*.

Philip. Good-bye, Comrade.

Dorothy. Comrade. Oh, and you said darling before.

Philip. Comrade's quite a word. I suppose I oughtn't to chuck it around. I take it back.

Dorothy. [*Rapturously*] Oh, Philip. *You're developing politically.*

Philip. God—er, oh you know, whatever it is, save us.

Dorothy. Don't blaspheme. It's frightfully bad luck.

Philip. [*Hurriedly and rather grimly*] Good-bye, *darling dear sweet*.

Dorothy. You don't call me *comrade*.

Philip. [*Going out*] No. You see I'm developing politically. [Pp. 24–25]

On his "true" side Philip is deadly serious about his mission. The instant transition he makes from drunken and irresponsible buffoon and bully to dedicated and sinister secret agent is jolting even to the reader (viewer) who is privy to it. Suddenly Philip confronts two guards who have allowed a fifth-column suspect to escape ("You're going to need a very good story indeed," p. 16), and he cautions harshly, "And there's only one thing about orders. THEY ARE TO BE OBEYED" (p. 18). Like the typical "Hemingway hero" that Philip Young claims Philip to be,[81] he is completely knowledgeable about his mission; of the fifth column, he says:

They have A numbered one to ten, and B numbered one to ten, and C numbered one to ten, and they shoot people and they blow up things and they do everything you're overly familiar with. And they work very hard, and aren't really awfully efficient. But they kill a lot of people that they shouldn't kill. The trouble is they've worked it out so well on the lines of the old Cuban A.B.C. that unless you get somebody outside that they deal with, it doesn't mean anything. It's just like cutting the heads off boils instead of listening to a Fleischmann's Yeast Program. [P. 36]

Philip, we gradually learn, has been in the spy business in Spain for twelve months, with experience in Cuba before that; he has apparently performed almost every kind of subterfuge except pimp ("That's about the only thing I haven't tried on this job," p. 43). Despite his certain knowledge that he will eventually be tortured, or worse ("It'll be a lot funnier face when I get through with this business," p. 58), Philip assumes this is to be his mission for life ("We're in for fifty years of undeclared wars and I've signed up for the duration," p. 80).

Philip shows Dorothy only one side of his life, the cynical devil-may-care side, which elicits from her a natural inclination to be frivolous herself, as well as a tendency to reform him ("Philip, you must promise me something. You won't just go on drinking and not have any aim in life and not do anything real?" p. 22). What is particularly unfair is that Philip has a secret and fanatically serious side and it is from that secret vantage point that he judges Dorothy. He first lures Dorothy into a pattern of behavior by assuming a completely false identity and allowing her to assume a false set of expectations. Then, on the basis of what he perceives as his "real" identity, he blames her for that very behavior. It is a most unfortunate kind of mental cheating: contrasted with his dedication to ridding the world of Fascism, her concern with clean boots; with glib analyses of the Madrid situation ("Everything's marvelous, now the heater's fixed," p. 5); with smuggling French food in Embassy pouches (unlike the "water soup" that the Spanish have available to them); her black-market pesetas and her silver fox cape ("Don't you want me to have *anything* nice-looking?" p. 61)—all seem tawdry and silly indeed.

To be fair one must acknowledge that Dorothy exhibits a marked tendency to be frivolous, even insensitive to the seriousness of the war she is in the middle of, and that this tendency would have been obvious, though probably somewhat less so, even if it had not been encouraged by Philip's "cover" behavior. She cultivates an irritating posture of coy ignorance from the beginning when she announces proudly, "I'm not typical Vassar. I didn't understand *anything* they taught me there" (p. 5). Not particularly admirable either are Dorothy's discussions with the maid Petra—Dorothy is served breakfast in bed, for example, by a woman who has had no breakfast at all; her glibly calling the shelling of the night before "lovely," after which Petra says, "in my quarter, there were six killed in one floor" (p. 20); and her ridiculous naivete about the fifth-column activity going on all around her: "You mean they shoot at people that they don't even know who they are?" (p. 46).

Far worse than Dorothy's naivete, however, are Philip's hypocrisy and capacity for violence. His hypocrisy is most obvious in that he never allows Dorothy to know the "rules" by which she is to be judged and in his continuing assurances that he loves her when he knows all along that he has committed the rest of his life to war against fascism, or against something ("I've signed on for the duration"). His break-off with Dorothy is thus unnecessarily cruel:

Philip. And have you ever been out to the Sans Souci in Havana on a Saturday night to dance in the Patio under the royal palms? They're gray and they rise like columns and you stay up all night there and play dice, or the wheel, and drive in to Jaimanitas for breakfast in the daylight. And everybody knows every one else and it's very pleasant and gay.

Dorothy. Can we go there?

Philip. No.

Dorothy. Why not, Philip?

Philip. We won't go anywhere.

Dorothy. Why not, darling?

Philip. You can go if you like. I'll draw you up an itinerary.

Dorothy. But why can't we go together?

Philip. You can go. But I've been to all those places and I've left them behind. And where I go now I go alone, or with others who go there for the same reason I go.

Dorothy. And I can't go there?

Philip. No.

Dorothy. And why can't I go wherever it is? I could learn and I'm *not* afraid.

Philip. One reason is I don't know where it is. And another is I wouldn't take you.

Dorothy. Why not?

Philip. Because you're useless, really. You're uneducated, you're useless, you're a fool and you're lazy. [P. 83]

When Carlos Baker says, "Philip's choice is between home and war—leaving Madrid with the girl or continuing to fight fascism,"[82] he seems to imply a more even balance between options than Philip ever really feels. Robert Lewis, Jr., seems closer to the mark when he says, "Philip Rawlings has, like Robert Jordan, committed himself to a cause which he admires, but the idea of brotherhood and freedom and its achievement through hatred and fear pose a dilemma for Philip."[83] Alfred Kazin, however, says it best, describing Philip as "a murdering gangster"; he goes on to say, "he was Jake Barnes making up for his impotence by murdering Fascists, and the Fascists were as unreal as the sick wisdom he and the perennial Lady Brett mumbled at each other in the midst of a civil war that was shaking Western society."[84]

We now have the advantage of historical hindsight to illuminate the fact that Franco's Fascists (and Mussolini's and Hitler's) ran almost a dead-heat with the Stalinists of Philip and

Max's persuasion in the destruction of human life and the devastation of basic principles of human decency. There is something sadly comic about Max's classic military rationale for the murderous enterprise he is a part of. He tells Philip: "You do it so *every one* will have a good breakfast like that. You do it so *no one* will ever be hungry. You do it so men will not have to fear ill health or old age; so they can live and work in dignity and not as slaves"; and "You do it to stop *that* [the shelling] forever"; and "You do it for all men. You do it for the children. And sometimes you do it even for dogs" (pp. 67–68). Thus the Stalinist Max, the man who wears his broken face like a military medal, voices the rationale uttered by most of the despots and their ideological thugs for at least the last two centuries.

The problem is that such humanistic mutterings stack up rather oddly against Philip's attitude toward the murder of Wilkinson. It is not the young man's death that bothers Philip so much as the fact that "that wasn't where I was going to use him" (p. 67)—implying that Wilkinson would have died either way. The idealism is at odds, too, with Philip's easy murder of the fat German officer ("He was too heavy and he would not walk," p. 74), and with his casual description of the torture of the captured Fascist politician:

Philip. Oh yes. I stayed all through it. Every bit of it. All of it. They needed to know something and they called me back.

Max. How was he?

Philip. Cowardly. But it only came out a little at a time for a while.

Max. And then?

Philip. Oh, and then finally he was spilling it out faster than a stenographer could take it. I have a strong stomach, you know.

Max. [*Ignoring this*] I see in the paper about the arrests. Why do they publish such things?

Philip. I don't know, my boy. Why do they? I'll bite.

Max. It is good for morale. But it is also very good to get every one. Did they bring in—the—ah—

Philip. Oh, yes. The corpse you mean? They fetched him in from where we left him, and Antonio had him placed in a chair in the corner and I put a cigarette in his mouth and lit it and it was all very jolly. Only the cigarette wouldn't stay lighted, of course.

Max. I am very happy I did not have to stay.

Philip. I stayed. And then I left. And then I came back. Then I left and they called me back again. I've been there until an hour ago and now I'm through. For today, that is. Finished my work for the day. Something else to do tomorrow. [Pp. 79–80]

Such scenes eradicate any distinction between the levels of indecency demonstrated by the opposing factions and they bring to mind journalist Sydney Harris' observation that the military figures of two sides of a conflict (and this would no doubt include secret agents as well) are almost invariably psychologically more compatible with each other than with the citizens of the side which they represent.

Whatever Dorothy's weaknesses, what she does seems decidedly preferable to what Philip and Max do. Despite Preston's view of her as a "bored Vassar bitch" (in much the same way that Cohn calls Brett Ashley "Circe"), Dorothy is not without positive attributes. She is "a tall handsome blonde girl" (p. 4); she appears genuinely to love Philip and to want to help him; she displays a courage during the shelling that surpasses that of Preston and the Spaniards; on one occasion she reveals that some of her frivolous behavior may, in fact, be a pose: "I'd like us to be married and work hard and have a fine life. You know I'm not as silly as I sound, or I wouldn't be here. And I work when you're not around" (p. 57)—the last claim attested to later when she says, "I've sent away three articles" (p. 82). Her behavior is certainly a substantial improvement over torturing politicians, propping up dead generals and putting cigarettes in their mouths, and spending your evenings for the next fifty years sneaking up on "the enemy" and shouting, like John Wayne, "Put your hands up and don't try anything heroic, or I'll blow your heads off" (p. 73).

IV

The "Minor" Women

One could profitably study any number of Hemingway's "minor" women, among them Mrs. Krebs, the "American lady" in "A Canary for One," and Sister Cecilia in "The Gambler, the Nun, and the Radio," but the seven "minor' women who seem to me most significant are Liz Coates, in "Up in Michigan," Marjorie in "The End of Something" and "The Three-Day Blow," Mrs. Elliot in "Mr. and Mrs. Elliot," Helen in "Cross-Country Snow," Jig in "Hills Like White Elephants," Mrs. Adams in "The Doctor and the Doctor's Wife" and "Now I Lay Me," and Prudence/Trudy in "Ten Indians" and "Fathers and Sons."[1]

LIZ COATES

Some of the "minor" women are accorded greater respect by both Hemingway and the critics than the most significant heroines, about whom much more has been written. Leon Linderoth, for example, includes Liz Coates in the category that he calls "the true Hemingway heroines"—the females who are most easily hurt, the naive, loving, trusting girls. They are easily identified by their long hair and their sweetly feminine ways—and by the way the world hurts them, usually through their lovers."[2] Naomi Grant, too, treats these women favorably: "Hemingway has a tacit sympathy with the women society neglects, looks down upon or wrongs. Liz Coates is one of the younger ones."[3] If I have any quarrel with the criticism on Liz Coates, it is principally isolated to the "psycho-technical" matter of her sexual "initiation." Arthur Waldhorn says of the experience that Liz has with Jim Gilmore: "Liz Coates is more nearly raped than seduced."[4] And John Aldridge says flatly, "Liz Coates had been raped."[5]

These interpretations oversimplify what is obviously a plethora of complicated and conflicting attitudes felt by Liz Coates and perhaps by most women experiencing sexual intercourse for the first time. The situation is age-old and would be trite as well if it did not represent such a poignant predicament in universal human experience. The young, inexperienced Liz, though she hardly knows him, "liked Jim very much"; Jim Gilmore, on the other hand, "liked her face because it was so jolly but he never thought about her" (p. 81). What human arrangement is more common?—the affection, only partly sexual, felt by a woman, contrasted with the almost exclusively physical attraction felt by a man. Even the perspective of the (obviously male) narrator focuses on the sexual; the earliest description reads, in part, "Liz had good legs and always wore clean gingham aprons" (p. 81).

Presumably these patterns of casual interest could have continued indefinitely if they had not been broken up by the deer-hunting trip. Because it separates the two, Jim returns in a "me-want-woman" state of mind, the archetypal man back from the hunt, and Liz accepts his sexual advances more readily than she otherwise would have. Jim's sexual enthusiasm (or lowered inhibitions) is intensified by his fatigue and his drinking: "Jim began to feel great. He loved the taste and the feel of whiskey" (p. 84). Shortly afterward, he advances directly toward his objective: "Jim came over back of her chair and stood there and she could feel him breathing and then he put his arms around her. Her breasts felt plump and firm and the nipples were erect under his hands. Liz was terribly frightened, no one had ever touched her, but she thought, 'He's come to me finally. He's really come' " (p. 84).

Despite her fear, Liz seems prepared to accept *some kind* of sexual activity ("she wanted it now"), because it will insure Jim's interest in her and because she herself is sexually stimulated. When Jim suggests a walk, she immediately accepts the offer. It seems apparent that Liz is not sure what the *it* is that she wants, though she is never deluded into thinking that it is something other than sexual: "She was very frightened and didn't know how he was going to go about things but she snuggled close to him" (p. 85). Liz's apprehensive aggressiveness (once again, "She was frightened but she wanted it. She had to have it but it frightened her," p. 85), rules out the rape thesis of Waldhorn and Aldridge, as well as Robert Lewis, Jr.'s, dictim that Hemingway's short stories "recurrently center on the theme of romantic illusions," [6] and Jackson Benson's interpretation that "instead of the 'martyr-victim,' Hemingway offers the girl who frankly enjoys sex and who is genuinely able to give herself, ungrudgingly, without a sense of sacrifice." [7]

There is much of the classic male-female struggle in the story. Liz, though not conveying a sense of sacrifice, does not frankly enjoy sex ("You mustn't do it, Jim. You mustn't," p. 85). There is, too—in confirmation of Naomi Grant's view of Hemingway's sympathy for women like Liz Coates—the almost stereotypic scene of female hurt and humiliation contrasted with male gratification and insensitivity: "The hemlock planks of the dock were hard and splintery and cold and Jim was heavy on her and he had hurt her. Liz pushed him, she was so uncomfortable and cramped. Jim was asleep. He wouldn't move" (p. 85). Pamella Farley calls this "the only realistic scene involving physical sex in the whole of Hemingway's published work." [8] The sense of disappointment is considerable: "Liz started to cry. . . . She was cold and miserable and everything felt gone" (p. 85). Liz is willing to accept some intimacy, perhaps a form of "petting" (though unfamiliar even with that kind of experience), but intercourse appears to exceed what she has anticipated.

The different sexual expectations of Liz and Jim may illustrate one of Alfred Kinsey's conclusions about the relationship between petting and social class: Petting, while an acceptable form of sexual activity for many women in all socioeconomic classes, including the lower class of which Liz is a part, is not acceptable to men of the lower classes, who typically involve themselves in no more than "a few minutes of hugging and kissing prior to actual coitus."[9] Whether Liz has expected only petting, or more than that, the story is one of disappointment, of male insensitivity to a traumatic moment in a woman's life, but not one of rape. There is not the requisite sense of violation or bitterness: "Liz leaned over and kissed him on the cheek. . . . Liz took off her coat and leaned over and covered him with it. She tucked it around him neatly and carefully" (pp. 85–86). The story shows exceptional sensitivity on Hemingway's part to the "woman's perspective" of that traumatic experience.

MARJORIE

Unlike Liz Coates, one of the few Hemingway women treated sympathetically by the critics, Marjorie, who appears in "The End of Something," and who is discussed in "The Three-Day Blow," is treated rather badly by almost everyone who has commented on the stories, although Leon Linderoth categorizes her, with Liz, as one of "the true Hemingway heroines."[10] John Killinger places her with Dorothy Bridges in the group of "bad" women, "who are demanding, who constrict the liberty of the heroes, who attempt to possess them."[11] Despite such observations, despite Philip Young's comment that many have complained that "The End of Something" has no "point"—a problem, he says, which occurs because "what point it does have is subtle and slight"[12]—the two stories and the character of Marjorie reveal something fundamental about the way a significant number of Hemingway's males treat women.

It is important here to distinguish between the male characters and Hemingway himself, the kind of author-subject distinction made early in every introductory literature course, but for some reason waived by most critics in the case of Hemingway. This waiver produces, even from luminaries like Leslie Fiedler, such woefully incomplete observations as "Hemingway is only really comfortable in dealing with 'men without women.' The relations of father to son, of battle-companions, friends on a fishing trip, fellow inmates in a hospital, a couple of waiters preparing to close up shop, a bullfighter and his manager . . . yet he feels an obligation to introduce women into his more ambitious fictions, though he does not know what to do with them beyond taking them to bed." [13] D. H. Lawrence comes closer to the truth of male-female relationships in Hemingway's short stories: "One wants to keep oneself loose. Avoid one thing only: getting connected up. Don't get connected up. If you get held by anything, break it. Don't be held. Break it, and get away." [14]

There is no other way to expain why Nick feels compelled to dump Marjorie. She seems everything the young outdoorsman would seek in a woman companion. Just as Helen in "The Snows of Kilimanjaro" can ride and shoot, so Marjorie (we learn in "The End of Something") can row a boat ("Nick and Marjorie rowed along the shore," p. 107), fish ("She loved to fish" and "Marjorie chased with her hands in the bucket, finally caught a perch, cut its head off and skinned it," p. 108), and, unlike the previously uninitiated Liz Coates, be completely at ease alone with Nick at night ("Marjorie went to the boat and brought a blanket . . . [she] sat on the blanket and waited for Nick," p. 109). She is everything that Hemingway admired in a woman and would later admire in his wife Mary. Those critics who read Nick as admirable (growing into manhood and all that) and Marjorie as "restricting" (merely echoing Nick's own perception) are not reading the words of the story carefully.

The immature Nick has grown tired of the relationship, or the obligation which it represents, and has planned this evening as the time to "disconnect." He acts strangely ("I don't feel like eating," p. 109); he is sarcastic ("You know everything," p. 110); he finally breaks off by saying, "It isn't fun any more. Not any of it" (p. 110).

After Marjorie inquires, "Isn't love any fun?" she remarks matter-of-factly, "I'm going to take the boat. . . . You can walk around the point" (p. 111). Despite critical charges that she "restricts" Nick, that she is "demanding," or "possessive"— or, in Lemuel Byrd's words, has a "debilitating effect on Nick"[15]—Marjorie is a notable female character. She is not guilty of any of those charges. She does not restrict Nick. She complements him in his interests ("Then Marjorie rowed the boat out over the channel-bank, holding the line in her teeth, and looking toward Nick, who stood on the shore holding the rod and letting the line run out from the reel"—pp. 108–109). She is neither demanding nor possessive: when Nick announces his loss of feeling for her, she makes one very logical inquiry ("Isn't love any fun?"), then simply and graciously leaves.

It is in "The Three-Day Blow" that Nick's friend Bill constructs for Nick a rationale for his break-off with Marjorie. On an afternoon of "man (or boy) talk" about whether "the Cards will ever win a pennant," about books, about getting drunk, about fishing and hunting, Bill explains: "You were very wise . . . to bust off that Marge business. . . . Once a man's married he's absolutely bitched." Immediately afterward Bill contradicts himself (partly because of the influence of the liquor, partly because he has no logical reason for saying what he did): "It was probably bad busting it off" (p. 122).

Aside from a vaguely unflattering reference to Marjorie's mother, it is apparent that Nick has no genuine reason for the break-off and now regrets it: "All he knew was that he had once had Marjorie and that he had lost her" (p. 123). The perspective here is Nick's alone, the concern only what *he* has lost—a "male perspective" shared by critics like Joseph DeFalco, who describes the split-up by saying that Nick "takes a positive course of action, and he alone must bear the brunt of its consequences."[16] Such a position completely overlooks the cost to Marjorie, who deserves better. It perpetuates a critical tendency (as with Wilson in "The Short Happy Life of Francis Macomber" and Harry in "The Snows of Kilimanjaro") to adopt toward a female character the negative attitudes of a male character whose own credibility is highly questionable. In the relationship between Nick and Marjorie, it is Nick who is weak, who is too immature to accept a love affair that shows no evidence of being restrictive, who is afraid of growing up, notwithstanding Bill's (and the critics') efforts to fabricate a rationale to relieve him of culpability.

MRS. ELLIOT

Treated even less sympathetically is Cornelia Elliot in "Mr. and Mrs. Elliot." Joseph DeFalco says of Mrs. Elliot and the other characters in the story that they "are more caricatures than characterizations."[17] Leon Linderoth says pointedly, "More malicious than Brett and Margaret Macomber, however, are such pure bitches as Mrs. Elliot." These "pure bitches"—a category which includes Mrs. Adams from the Nick Adams stories and Helene from *To Have and Have Not*—Linderoth continues, "seem to be total corrupters of the men with whom they associate,"[18] a familiar refrain for many of Hemingway's women, and, in the case of Mrs. Elliot and several of the Hemingway heroines already discussed in this work, an inaccurate one.

Both Mr. and Mrs. Elliot are sexual oddities and they come to each other in exactly that condition. Not only is Mr. Elliot "twenty-five years old and had never gone to bed with a woman until he married Mrs. Elliot," but he feels compelled to tell all of the girls that he dates that "he had led a clean [read: celibate] life" (p. 161). While Hubert Elliot has designed a rationale for his atypical sexual behavior ("He wanted to keep himself pure so that he could bring to his wife the same purity of mind and body that he expected of her," p. 161), his grasp of human realities is so slim that "he was shocked and really horrified at the way girls would become engaged to and marry men whom they must know had dragged themselves through the gutter" (pp. 161–62).

On Mrs. Elliot's side, the sexual activity is also atypical. Forty years old, she assumes the fundamentally sexless role of mother with Hubert, calling him "You dear sweet boy," because she "was pure too" (p. 162). Furthermore, heterosexual sex is intolerable to her ("They tried as often as Mrs. Elliot could stand it," p. 161), and she becomes joyful only when her "girl friend" comes to live with them ("Mrs. Elliot became much brighter after her girl friend came and they had many good cries together," p. 163; later, "Mrs. Elliot and the girl friend now slept together in the big medieval bed," p. 164).

Because their sexual activity together is so unsuccessful—on their wedding night she goes to sleep "disappointed," and, after she is asleep and he is stimulated by the shoes in the hotel hallway, he masturbates—they devise a way to rationalize the joylessness of their sexuality by explaining it as a mechanical act, which "Cornelia could not attempt . . . very often," made necessary because "they wanted a baby more than anything else in the world" (p. 163). It is not true but it provides them with the language, trite as it is, to deal with their own impotence during the transition period between the time they still feel obligated to perform the male-female sexual act, and the time, late in the story, when their sex roles are finally resolved comfortably. Hubert returns to living apart in "purity," (being busy, as he is, writing, and paying for the publication of, his poetry). Cornelia resumes the long-standing lesbian relationship with her girl friend.

It is strange to read the solemn criticisms of the story. Linderoth claims that Mrs. Elliot is a "pure bitch," and that she is a "total corrupter" of men; Pamella Farley finds that sexual love in the story "is founded on romantic notions of purity in love that are suitable for women but emasculate men." [19] For Mr. and Mrs. Elliot are serio-comic figures. Cornelia's "Oh-Dad-Poor-Dad" motherly fascination with Hubert's "purity" is a cause for bemusement, not alarm or condemnation, and Hubert's eagerness to avoid sex with his wife scarcely reflects the destruction of his masculinity by romantic notions of sexuality. The story gives no indication that he ever had any operating sexuality at all, a condition he conveniently covers with his "purity" ethic. Despite the irony of the closing line ("they were all quite happy," p. 164), in an odd way they all had what they wanted, and at no one's expense but their own.

HELEN

Treated as shabbily as Marjorie, and with as little legitimate reason, is the discussed, but never-seen, Helen in "Cross-Country Snow." Nick Adams and his companion George are enjoying a European skiing venture which will soon end because Nick must return to the United States to be with Helen, who is probably his wife but who is decidedly pregnant. It is obvious that the two men prefer their carefree ventures to George's obligation to return to school and Nick's obligation to return to Helen: "George and Nick were happy. They were fond of each other. They knew they had the run back home ahead of them." A moment later, in both language and thought characteristic of an adolescent, George says to Nick: "Gee, Mike, don't you wish we could just bum together? Take our skis and go on the train to where there was good running and then go on and put up at pubs and go right across the Oberland . . . and not give a damn about school or anything"—to which Nick answers, "Gee, the swell places" (p. 186).

Of these two obstacles, school for George and Helen for Nick, little is made of the former but much is made of the latter, especially by the critics. The two characters discuss Helen's pregnancy and its effect on Nick:

"Is Helen going to have a baby?" George said, coming down to the table from the wall.
"Yes."
"When?"
"Late next summer."
"Are you glad?"
"Yes. Now."
"Will you go back to the States?"
"I guess so."
"Do you want to?"
"No."
"Does Helen?"
"No."

George sat silent. He looked at the empty bottle and the empty glasses.
"It's hell, isn't it?" he said.
"No. Not exactly," Nick said.
"Why not?"
"I don't know," Nick said. [P. 187]

Here is confirmed D. H. Lawrence's interpretation of Hemingway's short-story heroes as individuals who, above all else, fear "getting connected up"; here is confirmed Leslie Fiedler's notion that in Hemingway there is the general "rejection of maturity and of fatherhood itself." [20] Immaturity is easy to understand, and so, as with Nick and Marjorie in "The End of Something," is irrational fear of responsibility, here compounded by the coming of the baby. Accepting that Nick is immature and irresponsible, we are not surprised by his answer that he does *not* wish to return to the States, nor by his answer that he "doesn't know" exactly how he feels about the whole situation. Like the Nick of "The End of Something," he has no reasons for his behavior, only "feelings" derived from a visceral urge not to "get connected up."

What is more difficult to understand is the critical interpretation of Helen "as letting down and trapping a man," [21] or as a woman who "cramps" a man's style, who "spoils her husband's idyll in the mountains with her undesired pregnancy." [22] Even if Arthur Waldhorn is right in asserting that Nick, like other Hemingway heroes, "seems to find that Eden without Eve is not only possible but preferable," [23] Nick can no longer claim that idyllic option since he did not prefer bed without Helen. It seems odd for readers and critics to join Nick in his self-serving view. The story is so morally skewed that Helen carries sole blame for the joint effort which produced her pregnancy. Worse, the pregnancy is seen as somehow conspiring with Helen to deny Nick the opportunity to play in the snow with his pal.

JIG

Hemingway shifts to a decidedly ''woman's perspective'' with the character Jig in ''Hills Like White Elephants.'' Theodore Bardacke may be right when he calls the story ''the most important story in relation to Hemingway's belief in the frustration of modern woman.''[24] H. E. Bates is almost certainly right when he says, ''For the girl something has crumpled up, and it is not only the past but the future. She is terrified, and the story is one of the most terrible Hemingway or anyone else ever wrote.''[25] The story *is* terrible, precisely because Hemingway, for the second time in the stories (he had allowed it in ''Up in Michigan''), allows the reader considerable access to the feelings of a woman at a traumatic moment in her life. This time a woman is confronted with a man who also wants ''to disconnect''—in this case, to disconnect from an unwanted child by pressing her into an abortion she does not want.

Unlike Marjorie, who accepts Nick's pronouncements and rows off quietly in the darkness, and unlike Helen, who, though consigned to a spoiler role is never seen, much less understood, Jig does protest and is both seen and understood. Moreover, the pettiness of the man, a judgment not confronted by the author in the case of Nick Adams, is amply demonstrated in one of the most quietly powerful scenes in all of Hemingway:

''It's really an awfully simple operation, Jig,'' the man said. ''It's not really an operation at all.''

The girl looked at the ground the table legs rested on.

''I know you wouldn't mind it, Jig. It's really not anything. It's just to let the air in.''

The girl did not say anything.

''I'll go with you and I'll stay with you all the time. They just let the air in and then it's all perfectly natural.''

''Then what will we do afterward?''

''We'll be fine afterward. Just like we were before.''

''What makes you think so?''

"That's the only thing that bothers us. It's the only thing that's made us unhappy."

The girl looked at the bead curtain, put her hand out and took hold of two of the strings of beads.

"And you think then we'll be all right and be happy."

"I know we will. You don't have to be afraid. I've known lots of people that have done it."

"So have I," said the girl. "And afterward they were all so happy."

"Well," the man said, "if you don't want to you don't have to. I wouldn't have you do it if you didn't want to. But I know it's perfectly simple."

"And you really want to?"

"I think it's the best thing to do. But I don't want you to do it if you don't really want to."

"And if I do it you'll be happy and things will be like they were and you'll love me?"

"I love you now. You know I love you."

"I know. But if I do it, then it will be nice again if I say things are like white elephants, and you'll like it?"

"I'll love it. I love it now but I just can't think about it. You know how I get when I worry."

"If I do it you won't ever worry?"

"I won't worry about that because it's perfectly simple." [P. 275]

This piece confirms D. H. Lawrence's judgment that "Mr. Hemingway's sketches . . . are excellent: so short, like striking a match, lighting a brief sensational cigarette, and it's over."[26] While Jig tries to distract herself by looking from the train station toward the hills which "look like white elephants," the insensitive and irresponsible man dishonestly diminishes the import of what he is asking of her: "It's really an awfully simple operation. . . . It's not really an operation at all. . . . It's really not anything"—a pathetically bald physiological argument which in no way takes into account the psychological devastation of a woman who does not wish to destroy her baby ("Doesn't it mean anything to you? We could get along," p. 277). More important, the woman suddenly sees the selfishness and hypocrisy of the man she has loved, a man, who with mock concern for her interests, can say: "You don't have to be afraid. I've known lots of people that have done it" and: "I wouldn't have you do it if you didn't want to. But I know it's perfectly simple" (p. 275) and: "I don't want you to do it if you don't want to. I'm perfectly willing to go through with it if it means anything to you" (p. 277).

It *is* a terrible story and it is Hemingway's most penetrating attack on man as the exploiter of woman. No punches are pulled: Out of sheer self-concern for the intrusion of a baby on his sexual and general pleasures, the man consciously devises an argument which never touches the basic concerns of the woman. She is considering killing someone that she wants to have and love, the impact such killing will have on her relationship with the man, and the hatred she has already started to feel for him, both because of the idea of the abortion and for his callous persistence in pressing it (all of this compounded by the moral milieu of the setting, a Catholic country fifty years ago). The man is arguing that there is no physical danger from the operation; that, following it, they will once again feel freedom in their relationship; that many people have such operations; that he will feel personally relieved (à la Nick Adams) to be rid of the added responsibility ("You know how I get when I worry," p. 275). One human relationship, in this case the one between the man and the woman, appears to be all most of Hemingway's males can sustain.

Caught up in making, *ad nauseam*, the case for the abortion and for his own freedom from responsibility, the man perceives neither the irony in Jig's responses nor the two things the irony means, Jig's hatred for him and her psychological destruction. Her early responses are bitter. She still has some control over herself psychologically, but her hatred for the man has already begun. When the man says that he has never seen a white elephant, she replies, "No, you wouldn't have" (p. 273). The bitterness gives way to further irony: He points out that many women have had abortions, to which she says, "And afterward they were all so happy" (p. 275). After his interminable talk about the "simple operation" which she begs him to stop, after he leaves briefly, returning to ask if she is feeling better, Jig has moved from active hatred of the man to the state of mental lethargy which signals a mind closing down in resignation. She smiles mindlessly at him and closes the story, saying, "I feel fine. . . . There's nothing wrong with me. I feel fine" (p. 278). She will have the abortion and shortly afterward their relationship will crumble, as will her mind. This is one of Hemingway's most poignant stories about the ways human beings selfishly (and often sexually) afflict one another.

MRS. ADAMS

The most widely treated of Hemingway's "minor" women is Nick Adams' mother, perhaps because of the long-standing critical fascination with Hemingway's relationships with his characters and the rather obvious fact that Mrs. Adams is modeled on Hemingway's own mother. Given Hemingway's description of his mother as "an all-time, All-American bitch," [27] it is little wonder that Leon Linderoth consigns Mrs. Adams and several other Hemingway women to the "pure bitch" category, noting that they "are treated entirely unsympathetically by [Hemingway]. He can find no saving grace about them. These women seem to be total corrupters of the men with whom they associate. [They] work constantly to unman their husbands in subtle ways . . . [and they] are alike in their unmitigated bitchery." [28]

If one takes the intended negative view of Mrs. Adams, the focus of interest in the story, "The Doctor and the Doctor's Wife," is in the final three pages. Dr. Adams, following his unsuccessful quarrel with Dick Boulton, returns to the cottage to find his wife in her room "with the blinds drawn" (p. 101). What emerges is the picture of a middle-aged hypochondriac, who is patronizingly righteous ("I hope you didn't lose your temper, Henry"; and "Remember, that he who ruleth his spirit is greater than he that taketh a city," p. 101)—what Naomi Grant aptly describes as the assumption of "moral and religious superiority." [29] Mrs. Adams, however, proves herself exceptionally naive and sensitive. When her husband explains that Boulton started the quarrel to avoid working out the debt he owes the doctor, she says, "Dear, I don't think, I really don't think that any one would really do a thing like that." When the doctor allows the door to slam as he leaves the cottage: "He heard his wife catch her breath when the door slammed" (p. 102).

Hemingway began building a case against Mrs. Adams in "The Doctor and the Doctor's Wife" and continued it in "Now I Lay Me." In the second story, set a few years later, as memories flood kaleidoscopically through Nick's insomniac mind, he recalls his mother cleaning out the basement of the Adams home ("designed and built by [Mrs. Adams]" p. 365) when Nick was a boy, and burning many of his father's cherished mementos:

About the new house I remember how my mother was always cleaning things out and making a good clearance. One time when my father was away on a hunting trip she made a good thorough cleaning out in the basement and burned everything that should not have been there. When my father came home and got down from his buggy and hitched the horse, the fire was still burning in the road beside the house. I went out to meet him. He handed me his shotgun and looked at the fire. "What's this?" he asked.

"I've been cleaning out the basement, dear," my mother said from the porch. She was standing there smiling, to meet him. My father looked at the fire and kicked at something. Then he leaned over and picked something out of the ashes. . . . He raked out stone axes and stone skinning knives and tools for making arrow-heads and pieces of pottery and many arrow-heads. They had all been blackened and chipped by the fire. My father raked them all out very carefully and spread them on the grass by the road. [Pp. 365–66]

Mrs. Adams is rendered as having a simple-minded but firm control over the home. In this instance she is described as burning "everything that should not have been there"—a thoughtless act based on a destructive attitude toward those things not important to her ("She was standing there smiling," p. 366). As Joseph DeFalco points out, this attitude, given her Christian Scientist views, could even ironically extend to a denial of the need for her husband's profession.[30] Others have tried to explain the unsynchronic relationship between Dr. and Mrs. Adams. Carlos Baker says ambiguously that "her temperament was as artistic as that of her husband was scientific,"[31] and Jackson Benson, more to the point, says that Dr. Adams is caught in "the trap created by a culture animated by the decadent remains of a Puritanism wherein patriarchy had given way to matriarchy."[32]

The other significant factor in the Adams domestic equation is Dr. Adams, who also has his vulnerable features, a point often overlooked by those eager to press the assault against his wife, and a point overlooked by Nick Adams (and perhaps Hemingway himself) until the later stories, particularly "Fathers and Sons." As early as "The Doctor and the Doctor's Wife," however, there are seeds of discontent about Dr. Adams. The doctor is at least partly vulnerable to Dick Boulton's tactless charge that he has stolen the logs which have washed ashore near his property. Though it was always possible that "the lumbermen *might* [my emphasis] never come" (p. 99) for the logs, we are also told: "They had drifted up onto the beach and if nothing were done about them sooner or later the crew of the *Magic* would come along the shore in a rowboat, spot the logs, drive an iron spike with a ring on it into the end of each one and then tow them out into the lake to make a new boom" (p. 99). Dr. Adams "always assumed" that the logs were being permanently abandoned, but in fact they were not. He was, as Boulton charges, taking property not his own.

Dr. Adams is vulnerable to a charge of cowardice as well. In "The Doctor and the Doctor's Wife," his cowardice is evident in his relationships with Dick Boulton and Mrs. Adams. Dr. Adams is goaded by Boulton about the drift logs: "Don't get huffy. I don't care who you steal from"   (p. 100). But, when the furious Dr. Adams tries to bluff Boulton down ("If you call me Doc once again, I'll knock your eye teeth down your throat," p. 101—the triteness of the threat suggestive of Dr. Adams' lack of familiarity with such an aggressive role), his bluff is called: " 'Oh, no, you won't, Doc'. . . . Dick Boulton looked at the doctor. Dick was a big man. He knew how big a man he was.

He liked to get into fights. He was happy." Dr. Adams has no choice but to back down: "The doctor chewed the beard on his lower lip and looked at Dick Boulton. Then he turned away and walked up the hill to the cottage" (p. 101).

In a minor confrontation with Mrs. Adams the doctor reveals his cowardice for the second time in the story. Against her patronizing admonitions ("I hope you didn't lose your temper") and her simple denials of his interpretation of the embarrassing events ("I can't really believe that any one would do a thing of that sort intentionally"), Dr. Adams once again fails to defend himself and instead simply walks away ("I think I'll go for a walk," p. 102). Much has been made of Mrs. Adams' escapist tendency to close herself away "in the darkened room" with her Bible and her Christian Science magazines. Dr. Adams, however, does much the same thing. He is quite inactive professionally, only occasionally attending to the medical needs of nearby Indians and allowing his medical journals to pile up "still in their wrappers unopened" (p. 101). As his wife withdraws to her dark room, he withdraws, often with Nick, to the sanctuary of the woods.

Dr. Adams' cowardice is demonstrated again in "Now I Lay Me," and Nick reflects on it years later in "Fathers and Sons." As earlier in "The Doctor and the Doctor's Wife," in "Now I Lay Me" Dr. Adams does not challenge his wife's thoughtlessness, but mildly succumbs to it. The fact that Mrs. Adams has "designed and built" the new house suggests that Dr. Adams has long since resigned himself to a subservient role. Nick's memory confirms this suspicion: After Mrs. Adams has burned the meaningful and probably valuable Indian relics, Dr. Adams responds merely by sending Nick for the rake, raking the relics out of the ashes, and remarking mildly, "The best arrow-heads went all to pieces" (p. 366).

In "Fathers and Sons" the full indictment of Dr. Adams—and, by implication, Dr. Hemingway—emerges. While Philip Young correctly states that Hemingway "started out rejecting his mother in defense of his father"[33] (an observation confirmed by the early stories), that attitude has changed by the late stories to reflect disrespect for his father as well. Hemingway described his mother as an "All-American bitch," but he also claimed "that the first big psychic wound of his life had come when he discovered that his father was a coward." [34] Mimi Gladstein places Mrs. Adams in a group with "Hemingway's mothers," as "illustrative of Philip Wylie's concept of 'momism,' a theory that saw the American female as emasculating, not allowing her male child to reach maturity." [35]

Gladstein's interpretation must be qualified by the fact that Mrs. Adams has very little influence on Nick from an early point in his life. He has opted for his father's companionship. At the close of "The Doctor and the Doctor's Wife," in response to his father's comment that Mrs. Adams wishes to see Nick, Nick says, "I want to go with you" (p. 103). The bitterness that Nick reveals in "Fathers and Sons" exists, not because his mother has not allowed him to "reach maturity" (he never assumed that she could), but because his father, on whom he depended completely, misled him on two fundamental issues, human sexuality and human courage. Dr. Adams was, as Nick describes him, "unsound on sex" (p. 490). Virtually every sexual activity fell into Dr. Adams' category of "heinous crime," including "mashing." Dr. Adams "had summed up the whole matter by stating that masturbation produced blindness, insanity, and death, while a man who went with prostitutes would contract hideous venereal diseases and that the thing to do was to keep your hands off of people" (p. 491). Whatever effect such extreme notions of sexuality had on the relationship between Dr. and Mrs. Adams, to Nick they represented, with his father's cowardice, a betrayal of the teacher-about-life role. Because of this betrayal, Nick remembers, "after he was fifteen he had shared nothing with him" (p. 496) ever again.

It is the cowardice, climaxed in Dr. Adams' suicide, which is most difficult for Nick to forgive, which makes it impossible for Nick to visit his father's grave, which causes Nick to think, at age thirty-eight, that he "could not write about him yet, although he would, later" (p. 490). Nick acknowledges that his father "had died in a trap that he had helped only a little to set" (pp. 489–90). He hints darkly of betrayal: "The handsome job the undertaker had done on his father's face had not blurred in his mind and all the rest of it was quite clear, including the responsibilities" (p. 491). (The full explanation of the father's suicide would not come until *For Whom the Bell Tolls*.) For now, we are left with a near-middle-age son who appears ready to forgive his father who, he feels, misled him badly (Nick says to his own son, in response to an observation about visiting Dr. Adams' grave: "We'll have to go. . . . I can see we'll have to go," p. 499). Mrs. Adams, on the other hand, for all the unflattering things written about her, was tuned out by her son so early in his life that she can hardly be said to have had any significant influence on him at all.

PRUDENCE/TRUDY

The last of Hemingway's significant "minor" women are Prudence and Trudy from "Ten Indians" and "Fathers and Sons." Though not a pressing issue, there is some confusion as to whether Nick Adams, as a youth, has two Indian girl friends, Prudence *and* Trudy, or whether, as Jackson Benson says, there is only one girl, with a variation of her name used in the second story: "Trudy—which, by the way, turns out to be the short form for Prudence and not Gertrude—turns up later in the Nick Adams chronology in 'Ten Indians.' " [36] It appears, however, that there *are* two girls. The character in "Ten Indians" is named Prudence *Mitchell* (p. 332), whereas the last name of the girl friend in "Fathers and Sons" is Gilby. Nick tells his son, "I went with a boy named Billy *Gilby* [my emphasis] and his sister Trudy" (p. 497). It seems unlikely that the difference in last names can be accounted for by either a step-brother/step-sister, or a half-brother/half-sister, relationship, for earlier in "Fathers and Sons" Nick recalls that *Eddie* Gilby "was their older half-brother" (p. 493). Since Nick makes this kind of distinction with Eddie, it seems unlikely that he would not have done the same for Billy and Trudy, if there were such a distinction to be made. Prudence Mitchell and Trudy Gilby are apparently different girls.

They are treated as one by some critics perhaps because their attitudes and sexual behavior are practically identical.

Too much has been made, in fact, of the issue of socio-sexual exploitation of the Indian girls by Nick, just as too much has been made of Hemingway's heroes' inability to have successful sexual relations with any women *except* the Indian girls. Edmund Wilson, most notably, is off the mark on both these issues: "The only women with whom Nick Adams' relations are perfectly satisfactory are the little Indian girls of his boyhood who are in a position of hopeless social disadvantage and have no power over the behavior of the white male—so that he can get rid of them the moment he has done with them."[37] This interpretation is reflected in the subsequent critical work of Theodore Bardacke, John Killinger, and Leon Linderoth. Bardacke says: "Nick . . . thinks back . . . to the one satisfying sexual relationship of the volume. This is an adolescent union with a little Indian girl who is submissive and devoid of any real individual personality";[38] Killinger claims that "Hemingway divides his women into the good and the bad, according to the extent to which they complicate a man's life. Those who are simple, who participate in relationships with the heroes and yet leave the heroes as free as possible, receive sympathetic treatment . . . [and into that] category fall the little Indian girls of the Nick Adams stories";[39] Linderoth says: "Perhaps the most clear-cut 'group' of Hemingway females would be the 'mindless Indian girls' . . . who demand nothing of a man, for they give nothing but their bodies."[40]

As inappropriate as the foregoing is Pamella Farley's blanket feminist statement: "In no piece of fiction or drama written by Hemingway is there a relationship between a man and a woman which is not degrading, including the idyllic romance genre where the woman is a cardboard slave existing solely to increase the stature of the man."[41] To all the critics quoted here, I would point out what only Leon Linderoth takes even brief account of— that, in "Ten Indians" and according to Nick's memory in "Fathers and Sons," Nick, Prudence, and Trudy are hardly more than children. Nick can be no older than his early teens, and the girls may be younger yet. They are only engaged in the innocent sexual experimentation of childhood ("Nick's own education in those earlier matters had been acquired in the hemlock woods behind the Indian camp," pp. 491–92).

Edmund Wilson's interpretation of the girls' "hopeless social disadvantage" and the "behavior of the white male" is too sociological. There is nothing in either story to suggest that Nick, or Prudence, or Trudy looks on their pleasures with any domination-submission notions of class consciousness at all, in spite of Carl's unflattering comparison, in "Ten Indians," between skunks and Indian girls ("Well, they smell about the same," p. 332). As to Wilson's idea that Nick can "get rid of" the Indian girls "the moment he had done with them," it is not borne out by the stories. The eventual separation of Nick and Trudy in "Fathers and Sons" is unexplained, but the following conversation between Nick and his father in "Ten Indians" clearly suggests that Prudence "has done with" Nick:

"I saw your friend, Prudie."
"Where was she?"
"She was in the woods with Frank Washburn. I ran onto them. They were having quite a time."
His father was not looking at him.
"What were they doing?"
"I didn't stay to find out."
"Tell me what they were doing."
"I don't know," his father said. "I just heard them threshing around."
"How did you know it was them?"
"I saw them."
"I thought you said you didn't see them."
"Oh, yes, I saw them."
"Who was it with her?" Nick asked.
"Frank Washburn."
"Were they—were they—"
"Were they what?"
"Were they happy?"
"I guess so." [P. 335]

To Theodore Bardacke I would point out that Trudy is hardly either "submissive" or "devoid of any real individual personality." In "Fathers and Sons," Trudy is quite aggressive in her sexual activity, even childishly shameless. When Nick suggests that they go away from Billy for their pleasures, Trudy says, "No, here. . . . I no mind Billy. He my brother" (p. 493). Afterward, when Nick is sated, Trudy becomes the initiator of still further sexual activity: "She put her hand in Nick's pocket. . . . Trudy was exploring with her hand in Nick's pocket." She says, "You want to do anything now?" (p. 494)—and indeed they do, after which "Trudy folded her brown legs together happily and rubbed against him" (p. 495). Trudy is certainly not submissive and the childish libertinism which makes up much of her character provides considerable "individual personality."

I would respond to John Killinger's interpretation of the Indian girls as falling in the category of "good women" because they do not "complicate a man's life," to Leon Linderoth's explanation that the Indian girls "demand nothing of a man, for they give nothing but their bodies," and to Pamella Farley's assumption that Nick's relationships with the Indian girls, like all other relationships in Hemingway "between a man and a woman," are "degrading," by pointing out that both the expressions and the concepts of "man" and "woman" are inappropriate for dealing with these three characters. Nick is a young boy, and Prudence and Trudy are young girls and, as such, they have little but their bodies to give to each other. Killinger and Farley particularly, like many critics categorizing Hemingway's men and women, fail to make adequate distinction between the quite equally balanced contributions made to, and gratification received from, the innocent sexual experimentation of the three children, and the socio-politics—with the class consciousness and potential for irresponsibility and exploitation which that implies—which is indeed part of the adult sexuality of some Hemingway characters.

Such a distinction is especially critical in treating Hemingway. When Nick Adams, at age thirty-eight in "Fathers and

Sons," remembers his childhood experience with Trudy ("Could you say she did first what no one has ever done better and mention plump brown legs, flat belly, hard little breasts, well holding arms, quick searching tongue, the flat blue eyes, the good taste of mouth," p. 497), it does not mean that he can handle sex only with "inferiors," and not with "real adult women," therefore that he is not a "man." He implies, for himself as well as for most of Hemingway's adult male characters, that relationships with females (particularly sexual relationships) can never really be entered into freely after childhood, because for children (even adolescents), there are no serious encumbrances to interfere with the relationships. From young manhood on, as we see with Nick Adams, and with Frederick Henry, Harry Morgan, Philip Rawlings, Robert Jordan, and Richard Cantwell, such relationships can never again be free and completely enjoyable. The men have a near-pathological fear of accepting the responsibility which "getting connected up" automatically brings. For Hemingway's men, success in life (or "manhood") is far more often and more seriously measured by the man's unswerving devotion to a "mission" (usually played out on a testing ground of violence and destruction)—what Carlos Baker calls "a preoccupation with the work a man must do, where women have no place and may even be in the way" [42]—than by the man's capacity for such humanistic endeavors as loving a woman for a sustained period of time.

V

Hemingway the Man— and the Writer

The orthodoxy of beliefs about Hemingway's life, especially his attitudes toward "manhood" and violence, has been consistently applied on virtually a one-to-one basis to the male characters of his stories, novels, and play. Hemingway's obsessively public celebration of himself and his wartime and sportsman exploits make such a transfer tempting, of course. Critics have been routinely making this transfer for the last forty years, but it renders the motives and actions of his fictional characters more transparent than the actual language of the stories and novels proves them to be. The major distinction between Hemingway the man and Hemingway the writer is that the man never really grew up, whereas the writer did.

HEMINGWAY'S VIEWS OF "MANHOOD"

There was something pathetic about so talented and sound a writer having continually to pound his barrel chest for all the world to see, to announce to friends and enemies alike what manhood really was. "Real men" never, as he blustered about Henry James' male characters, talk "like fairies."[1] They never take rejection "lying down"; when Agnes von Kurowsky, on whom Catherine Barkley was partly modeled, refused Hemingway's offer of marriage, he wrote to a friend that he hoped when Agnes returned to the United States "she would trip on the gangplank and bust all her goddamned teeth."[2] When Gertrude Stein accused Hemingway, in her memoirs, of being "yellow," he bitterly told friends that Stein "had decided that nobody was any good who was not queer."[3]

As an avowed "real man," Hemingway lined the walls of his homes with photographs of himself and his "kills," and with the heads of animals he had shot.[4] He described in detail how, while in China, he ate "monkey brains right out of the monkey's skull."[5] He talked of the "rough and dirty" boyhood he had had the strength to overcome[6] and he affirmed his "manhood" through his boxing skills, both in the ring and outside bars, as the unfortunate Wallace Stevens (and later some critics) learned:

Wallace Stevens, a tall, gray man of portly build who was both an executive in a Hartford insurance company and one of the best poets then writing in the United States, had come to Key West for a short vacation. Stevens was a complete novice in boxing, besides being twenty years Hemingway's senior. For reasons that remain obscure, the poet seems to have baited the novelist into some sort of fight. Stevens emerged with a black eye and a badly bruised face. Waldo Pierce saw him next day, wearing dark glasses to conceal the damage. Stevens understandably asked Hemingway to say nothing publicly about the affair. Although Ernest complied, since he admired and respected Stevens as a poet, he could not resist an oblique and tantalizing reference in a letter to Dos Passos.[7]

Hemingway met quite fully the three criteria Sheldon Grebstein outlines for male "toughness:" 1. "sheer physical stamina and the ability . . . to keep functioning despite pain and bodily damage"; 2. "control over personal feeling and natural appetites, especially in a professional situation"; 3. "the power to confront death without morbid pessimism or specious piety."[8] There seems to be rather general agreement among critics and biographers alike, however, that the key to understanding why Hemingway defined "manhood" as he did is to be found in the third of these criteria—his attitude toward death.

Philip Young maintains that Hemingway ''overexposed'' himself to those things that he feared, chief among them death.[9] Such an interpretation fits a larger, cogent Freudian explanation of one manner of dealing with something dreadfully feared: to immerse oneself completely in the milieu in which the feared thing exists (war, for example, or dangerous hunting, if the fear is of death) so that the individual is relieved of the fear by being in constant contact with the feared thing yet not being affected by it, or by being destroyed by the thing feared and thus ironically being freed from it. Deming Brown takes a more comprehensive view of Hemingway's fear of death: ''But the obsession with death was only part of a larger composite of desolation in Hemingway. Accompanying this morbid, vigorous probing at the ultimate terror was a feeling of futility, an all-embracing attitude of indifference and passivity.''[10]

However comprehensive or intense Hemingway's fear of death was, his way of dealing with it was to stride boldly into the milieu of threatened death and, by being strong and stoic, by doing the job which ''must be done,'' by ''being a man,'' to achieve temporary victory over that feared thing hovering so close. Lincoln Kirstein put it this way: ''Mr. Hemingway believes in the courage of immediate physical action above all other.''[11] Edgar Johnson says: ''But momentarily Hemingway [tried] to ignore the implication that the only separate peace is in death. He [would] solve the problem of dealing with the world by taking refuge in individualism and isolated personal relationships and sensations.''[12]

HEMINGWAY'S ATTRACTION TO VIOLENCE

There has been much effort to link Hemingway's sense of ''manhood'' with his association with violence—Alfred Kazin described Hemingway as a ''dilettante of violence.''[13] Much of that linkage is valid, but some critics have waxed too philosophical on the issue, particularly in attempts to show that Hemingway's vision of the world, because it was violent, was more ''natural,'' or honest. Wyndham Lewis calls Hemingway ''the Noble Savage of Rousseau, but a white version, the simple

American man'';[14] Mario Praz implies that what Hemingway offers is "a return to nature [which] has been, every now and then, the infallible remedy for a too sophisticated society";[15] and Ivan Kashkeen tells us that "war made Hemingway see death without disguise or heroic illusions."[16]

To Praz particularly, I would respond that sometimes something ennobling can indeed come from a "return to nature," but only when it is the noble elements of nature that one returns to—the elements of pride in earth and its products, and affection for nature's creatures, including human beings. The nature that Hemingway returned to repeatedly was the nature of barbarism, which shows only occasional concern for the products and aesthetics of the earth and little at all for its animal and human inhabitants, both of which were depleted at a substantial rate in the environments in which he chose to spend most of his life. This is clearly not the "nature" of Ceres but instead the "nature" of Moloch, with the accoutrements of technology added. It is the nature of "turf" consciousness, in which the powerful and the corrupt, in their classic warrior roles, eagerly destroy—and destroy for—other people's "turfs."

To Kashkeen's observation that Hemingway came to see "death without disguise or illusions," I reply that, while Hemingway, as various critics have claimed, may have rightly attacked the hypocrisies of latent Victorian pretentiousness and morality, his life contributed to a form of hypocrisy far more harmful. He extended the unfortunate human instinct for violence into a ritual by which individuals (notably men) measure their "courage" and their value generally. Such rituals are forms of both "disguise" and "heroic illusions." They require, in the absence of circumstantial violence (like wars and social upheavals, which are caused by the convergence of forces and political leverage over which individuals and small groups of individuals have no control), the continual manufacture of individual and small-group forms of violence for proving manhood.

The preference of Hemingway for violence over affection, to show that he had *cojones*, is a preference as old as mankind. Psychiatrist Eric Berne says:

It is important to realize that certain "genocidal" aspects of human nature have remained unchanged during the past five thousand years regardless of any genetic evolution which has taken place during this period; they also remain immune to environmental and social influences. One of these is the prejudice against darker people which has persisted unchanged since the dawn of recorded time in ancient Egypt, whose "miserable people of Cush" are still represented in oppressed Negro populations throughout the world. The other is "search and destroy" warfare. For example:

"234 Viet Cong ambushed and killed" and "237 villagers slaughtered in Viet Nam." (Both from U. S. Army reports, 1969)

Compare: "800 of their soldiers by my arms I destroyed; their populace in the flames I burned; their boys, their maidens, I dishonored. 1000 of their warriors' corpses on a hill I piled up. On the first of May, I killed 800 of their fighting men, I burned their many houses, their boys and maidens I dishonored," etc. (From the Annals of Assur-Nasir-Pal, Column II, about 870 B.C.E.)

Thus for at least 2800 years there have been willing and eager corpse-counters. The good guys end up as "casualties"; the bad guys as "bodies," "dead," or "corpses." [17]

Whether one views Hemingway's manhood-violence instincts psychologically, as Philip Young does when he calls them "traumatic neuroses," a "death instinct" which requires that an individual kill other things, vicariously or actually, in order not to kill himself;[18] socially, as does John Aldridge, who speaks of "the chest-beating, wisecracking pose that was later to seem so incredibly absurd";[19] or emotionally, as does Dwight Macdonald, who says that "Hemingway was adolescent all his life,"[20] they were instincts that were an open and generally agreed upon part of Hemingway the man.

HEMINGWAY THE WRITER

But what about Hemingway the writer? Can we make the same charges? Were these same instincts injected into the Hemingway heroes one-for-one? Were Nick Adams, Jake Barnes (without the "handicap"), Frederick Henry, Harry Morgan, Robert Jordan,

Philip Rawlings, Robert Wilson, Harry ("Kilimanjaro"), even
the aging Cantwell and Santiago merely thin disguises for Hemingway
the man? Most critics who have treated Hemingway's
fiction have automatically assumed that they generally were. Mark
Schorer says: "[Hemingway] pressed his style into the service
of his subject matter in a rather special way: the style was the
immediate representation of the moral attitude of the author toward
his material, it objectified the author's values and thus in
itself was comment in writing otherwise unhampered by comment."[21] Later he added, "Courage stylized, *style*, then, matters
finally."[22] John Killinger explains Hemingway's heroes as
experiencing existential rebirth: "The Hemingway hero, reincarnate
in each of his wounded strong men from Nick Adams to
the old fisherman Santiago, passes through the experience of
violence into a world that is invariably simpler than the one from
which he has come."[23] Carlos Baker claims that Hemingway
"became the pragmatic moralist whose leading aim was to find
out how to live in life . . . [and] how to convert a carefully
cultivated stoical fortitude into the stuff of which his fictional
heroes were made."[24]

This is tempting stuff all right. Observe the autobiographical
similarities: Nick Adams fishing in Michigan as Hemingway did
(and hating his parents just as much); Frederick Henry having
his knee blown away like Hemingway; Robert Wilson and his
protege Macomber hunting lions and buffalo in Africa; the dying
Harry hunting Kilimanjaro; Santiago fishing off Cuba; and on
and on. But this is the normal stuff of fiction. Every writer uses
familiar settings, activities, and human qualities. Hemingway *does*
draw his characters closer to himself than some writers, but many
others do the same without being charged with creating themselves
in their characters.

Hemingway, in other words, must be read with the same respect
that freshman literature students are taught to offer any author.
They learn to ask, "What does the story *say*?" They learn
that if the omniscient narrator seems reliable, *believe the words
of the narrator*. They learn that characters must be assumed *to
speak for themselves*, not for the author, and that they *are*

speaking for themselves when they make judgments about themselves or about other characters.

In the case of Hemingway, the critics, besides being consistently overzealous in believing each other, have eagerly believed the judgments of characters who show every evidence, in Hemingway's own words, that they should not be trusted, that they should not be considered *to be* Hemingway. The masochism of Jake Barnes is a form of weakness Hemingway could hardly have admired, though Jake's stoicism is something that he could. Most of the heroes have similar qualities of stoicism and determination to do their work well, but most also have qualities that Hemingway did not respect: the sadism of Harry Morgan (glibly telling about cracking Mr. Sing's voice box with his thumbs) and Philip Rawlings (casually torturing, mutilating, Fascists for frequently useless information; the criminality of the guide Robert Wilson (hunting illegally and making himself an accessory to murder in order to defeat a woman he does not like); the foolishness of Robert Jordan (who continues a doomed mission at the cost of his own and many other lives). Similar, though less dramatic, cases can be made against accepting the values of Nick Adams, Cantwell, and others as Hemingway's, too.

One of the most unfortunate results of the excessive time critics have spent defining Hemingway's philosophy of "manhood" and violence, and in devising parallels between Hemingway and his heroes, is that so little serious consideration has been given to the women. Most of the time they have been written off as small parts of some simplistic formula. From the penetrating and compelling portrayals of female trauma found in Liz Coates ("Up in Michigan"), Jig ("Hills Like White Elephants"), Catherine Barkley, Helen ("Kilimanjaro"), even Brett Ashley, to the victimized women like Marjorie ("The End of Something"), Helen ("Cross-Country Snow"), Dorothy Bridges, even Margot Macomber, to the deeply loving women like Marie Morgan, the Spanish Maria and Renata, Hemingway has presented interesting, dramatic characters, who offer a vision of life that is more humane and decent than that offered by the "heroes" with whom they spend—and often waste—their lives.

Notes

PREFACE

1. Dwight Macdonald, *Against the American Grain* (New York: Random House, 1962), p. 171.

2. Philip Young, *Ernest Hemingway* (New York: Rinehart, 1952), p. 124.

3. Leicester Hemingway, *My Brother, Ernest Hemingway* (New York: World, 1962), p. 15.

I. HEMINGWAY, THE WOMEN, AND THE CRITICS

1. Delmore Schwartz, "Ernest Hemingway's Literary Situation," *Ernest Hemingway: The Man and His Work*, ed. John K. M. McCaffery (New York: Avon, 1950), p. 107.

2. Maxwell Geismar, *American Moderns: From Rebellion to Conformity* (New York: Hill and Wang, 1958), p. 59.

3. Philip Young, *Ernest Hemingway* (New York: Rinehart, 1952), p. 124.

4. Joseph Warren Beach, *American Fiction 1920–1940* (New York: Russell and Russell, 1960), p. 69.

5. Michael F. Moloney, "Ernest Hemingway: The Missing Third Dimension," *Hemingway and His Critics: An International Anthology*, ed. Carlos Baker (New York: Hill and Wang, 1961), p. 180.

6. Conrad Aiken, "Expatriates," *The Merrill Studies in The Sun Also Rises*, ed. William White (Columbus, Ohio: Charles E. Merrill, 1969), p. 3.

7. Malcolm Cowley, "A Portrait of Mister Papa," *Ernest Hemingway: The Man and His Work*, ed. John K. M. McCaffery (New York: Avon, 1950), p. 47.

8. Carlos Baker, *Ernest Hemingway: A Life Story* (New York: Scribner's, 1969), p. x.

9. Philip Young, *Ernest Hemingway: A Reconsideration* (University Park: Pennsylvania State University Press, 1966), p. viii.

10. Maxwell Geismar, *American Moderns*, p. 64.

11. John W. Aldridge, *After the Lost Generation: A Critical Study of the Writers of Two Wars* (New York: McGraw-Hill, 1951), pp. 23–25.

12. Carlos Baker, *Ernest Hemingway: A Life Story*, p. 187.

13. Leon Edel, "The Art of Evasion," *Hemingway: A Collection of Critical Essays*, ed. Robert P. Weeks (Englewood Cliffs, N.J.: Prentice-Hall, 1962), p. 169.

14. Dwight Macdonald, *Against the American Grain* (New York: Random House, 1962), p. 173.

15. Ibid., pp. 167–70.

16. Ibid., p. 171.

17. Ibid., p. 180.

18. George Plimpton, "An Interview with Ernest Hemingway," *Hemingway and His Critics*, ed. Carlos Baker (New York: Hill and Wang, 1961), p. 32.

19. Carlos Baker, *Ernest Hemingway: A Life Story*, p. 475.

20. Philip Young, *Ernest Hemingway: A Reconsideration*, p. 6.

21. Dwight Macdonald, *Against the American Grain*, p. 171.

22. George Plimpton, "Interview," p. 26.

23. Ibid., p. 27.

24. Ibid., p. 29.

25. Carlos Baker, *Ernest Hemingway: A Life Story*, p. 509.

26. Mary Welsh Hemingway, *How It Was* (New York: Knopf, 1976), pp. 298–99.

27. George Plimpton, "Interview," p. 24.

28. Carlos Baker, *Ernest Hemingway: A Life Story*, p. 219.

29. Ibid., p. 320.

30. Maxwell Geismar, *American Moderns*, p. 54.

31. Carlos Baker, *Ernest Hemingway: A Life Story*, p. 317.

32. Theodore Bardacke, "Hemingway's Women," *Ernest Hemingway: The Man and His Work*, ed. John K. M. McCaffery (New York: Avon, 1950), p. 307.

33. Philip Young, *Ernest Hemingway*, p. 81.

34. Arthur Waldhorn, *A Reader's Guide to Ernest Hemingway* (New York: Farrar, Straus and Giroux, 1972), p. 123.

35. Jackson J. Benson, *Hemingway: The Writer's Art of Self-Defense* (Minneapolis: University of Minnesota Press, 1969), p. 29.

36. John Killinger, *Hemingway and the Dead Gods: A Study in Existentialism* (Lexington: University of Kentucky Press, 1960), p. 89.

37. Pamella Farley, "Form and Function: The Image of Woman in Selected Works of Hemingway and Fitzgerald" (Ph.D. diss., Pennsylvania State University, 1973), p. 30.

38. Lionel Trilling, "An American in Spain," *Ernest Hemingway: Critiques of Four Major Novels*, ed. Carlos Baker (New York: Scribner's, 1962), p. 81.

39. André Maurois, "Ernest Hemingway," *Hemingway and His Critics*, ed. Carlos Baker (New York: Hill and Wang, 1961), p. 51.

40. Sharon Welch Dean, "Lost Ladies: The Isolated Heroine in the Fiction of Hawthorne, James, Fitzgerald, Hemingway, and Faulkner" (Ph.D. diss., University of New Hampshire, 1973), p. 126.

41. Leon Linderoth, "The Female Characters of Ernest Hemingway" (Ph.D. diss., Florida State University, 1966), pp. 105ff.

42. Leslie A. Fiedler, *Love and Death in the American Novel* (New York: Criterion, 1960), p. 304.

43. Ibid., p. 304.

44. Donald Heiney, *Recent American Literature* (Woodbury, N.Y.: Barron's Educational Series, 1958), p. 149.

45. Ibid., p. 148.

II. CASSANDRA'S DAUGHTERS

1. Dwight Macdonald, *Against the American Grain* (New York: Random House, 1952), p. 176.

2. B. E. Todd, "A Review of *A Farewell to Arms*," *The Merrill Studies in A Farewell to Arms*, ed. John Graham (Columbus, Ohio: Charles E. Merrill, 1971), p. 23.

3. Clifton P. Fadiman, "A Review of *A Farewell to Arms*," *The Merrill Studies in A Farewell to Arms*, ed. John Graham (Columbus, Ohio: Charles E. Merrill, 1971), p. 20.

4. Malcolm Cowley, "A Portrait of Mister Papa," *Ernest Hemingway: The Man and His Work*, ed. John K. M. McCaffery (New York: Avon, 1950), p. 26.

5. W. M. Frohock, *The Novel of Violence in America* (Dallas: Southern Methodist University Press, 1957), p. 195.

6. Samuel Shaw, *Ernest Hemingway* (New York: Frederick Ungar, 1973), p. 62.

7. Arthur Waldhorn, *A Reader's Guide to Ernest Hemingway* (New York: Farrar, Straus, and Giroux, 1972), p. 123.

8. Otto Friedrich, "Ernest Hemingway: Joy Through Strength," *The Merrill Studies in A Farewell to Arms*, ed. John Graham (Columbus, Ohio: Charles E. Merrill, 1971), p. 48.

9. Philip Young, *Ernest Hemingway* (New York: Rinehart, 1952), pp. 62–63.

10. Dwight Macdonald, *Against the American Grain*, p. 176.

11. *A Farewell to Arms* was originally published in New York by Scribner's in 1929. All page references apply to the 1929 edition.

12. Wyndham Lewis, "The 'Dumb Ox' in Love and War," *Twentieth Century Interpretations of A Farewell to Arms*, ed. Jay Gellens (Englewood Cliffs, N.J.: Prentice-Hall, 1970), p. 76.

13. Carlos Baker, *Ernest Hemingway: A Life Story* (New York: Scribner's, 1969), p. 38.

14. Frederick J. Hoffman, *The Twenties: American Writing in the Postwar Decade* (New York: The Free Press, 1965), p. 72.

15. J. F. Kobler, "Let's Run Catherine Barkley Up the Flag Pole and See Who Salutes," *CEA Critic* (January, 1974), pp. 4–5.

16. Leslie A. Fiedler, *Love and Death in the American Novel* (New York: Criterion, 1960), p. 306.

17. Joseph Warren Beach, *American Fiction: 1920–1940* (New York: Russell and Russell, 1960), p. 84.

18. Otto Friedrich, "Ernest Hemingway," p. 48.

19. Raymond A. Moody, Jr., *Life after Life* (New York: Bantam, 1976), p. 92.

20. Naomi M. Grant, "The Role of Women in the Fiction of Ernest Hemingway" (Ph.D. diss., University of Denver, 1969), pp. 96–97.

21. Wyndham Lewis, "The 'Dumb Ox,' in Love and War," p. 76.

22. W. M. Frohock, *The Novel of Violence*, p. 176.

23. Pier Francesco Paolini, "The Hemingway of the Major Works,"

Hemingway and His Critics: An International Anthology, ed. Carlos Baker (New York: Hill and Wang, 1961), p. 133.

24. Arthur Waldhorn, *A Reader's Guide*, p. 22.

25. Elliot Paul, "Hemingway and the Critics," *Ernest Hemingway: The Man and His Work*, ed. John K. M. McCaffery (New York: Avon, 1950), p. 98.

26. Alvah C. Bessie, "Review of *For Whom the Bell Tolls*," *Ernest Hemingway: Critiques of Four Major Novels*, ed. Carlos Baker (New York: Scribner's, 1962), p. 91.

27. Delmore Schwartz, "Ernest Hemingway's Literary Situation," *Ernest Hemingway: The Man and His Work*, ed. John K. M. McCaffery (New York: Avon, 1950), p. 107.

28. See Deming Brown, "Hemingway in Russia," *Hemingway and His Critics: An International Anthology*, ed. Carlos Baker (New York: Hill and Wang, 1961). Also see Sheldon Norman Grebstein, "The Tough Hemingway and His Hard-Boiled Children," *Tough Guy Writers of the Thirties*, ed. David Madden (Carbondale: Southern Illinois University Press, 1968).

29. Edgar Johnson, "Farewell the Separate Peace," *Ernest Hemingway: The Man and His Work*, ed. John K. M. McCaffery (New York: Avon, 1950), p. 122.

30. Joseph Warren Beach, *American Fiction*, p. 69.

31. Carlos Baker, *Ernest Hemingway: A Life Story*, p. 287.

32. Samuel Shaw, *Ernest Hemingway*, p. 92.

33. Philip Young, *Ernest Hemingway* (Minneapolis: University of Minnesota Press, 1959), p. 14.

34. Delmore Schwartz, "Ernest Hemingway's Literary Situation," p. 108.

35. *To Have and Have Not* was originally published in New York by Scribner's in 1937. All page references apply to the 1937 edition.

36. Wyndham Lewis, "The 'Dumb Ox,' " p. 73.

37. Eric Berne, *What Do You Say After You Say Hello? The Psychology of Human Destiny* (New York: Grove, 1972), pp. 268–69.

38. Lincoln Kirstein, "The Canon of Death," *Ernest Hemingway: The Man and His Work*, ed. John K. M. McCaffery (New York: Avon, 1950), p. 49.

39. Edmund Wilson, *The Wound and the Bow* (Cambridge: Houghton Mifflin, 1941), p. 238.

40. Ibid., p. 230.

41. Theodore Bardacke, "Hemingway's Women," *Ernest Hemingway: The Man and His Work*, ed. John K. M. McCaffery (New York: Avon, 1950), p. 315.

42. Leon W. Linderoth, "The Female Characters of Ernest Hemingway" (Ph.D. diss., Florida State University, 1966), p. 62.

43. Joseph Warren Beach, *American Fiction*, p. 79.

44. Pier Francesco Paolini, "The Hemingway of the Major Works," p. 133.

45. Elliot Paul, "Hemingway and the Critics," p. 96.

46. Carlos Baker, *Ernest Hemingway: A Life Story*, p. 385.

47. Mark Schorer, "The Background of a Style," *Ernest Hemingway: Critiques of Four Major Novels*, ed. Carlos Baker (New York: Scribner's, 1962), p. 89.

48. W. M. Frohock, *The Novel of Violence*, p. 176.

49. Dwight Macdonald, *Against the American Grain*, p. 168.

50. Theodore Bardacke, "Hemingway's Women," p. 316.

51. Maxwell Geismar, "Ernest Hemingway: You Could Always Come Back," *Ernest Hemingway: The Man and His Work*, ed. John K. M. McCaffery (New York: Avon, 1950), p. 165.

52. Sharon Dean, "Lost Ladies: The Isolated Heroine in the Fiction of Hawthorne, James, Fitzgerald, Hemingway, and Faulkner" (Ph.D diss., University of New Hampshire, 1973), p. 129.

53. Samuel Shaw, *Ernest Hemingway*, p. 101.

54. See Raymond A. Moody, Jr., *Life after Life* (New York: Bantam, 1976).

55. *For Whom the Bell Tolls* was originally published in New York by Scribner's in 1940. All page references apply to the 1940 edition.

56. Maxwell Geismar, "Ernest Hemingway: You Could Always Come Back," p. 165.

57. Philip Young, *Ernest Hemingway* (New York: Rinehart, 1952), p. 80.

58. Ivan Kashkeen, "Alive in the Midst of Death: Ernest Hemingway," *Hemingway and His Critics: An International Anthology*, ed. Carlos Baker (New York: Hill and Wang, 1961), p. 169.

59. W. M. Frohock, *The Novel of Violence*, p. 195.

60. Mimi Reisel Gladstein, "The Indestructible Woman in the Works of Faulkner, Hemingway, and Steinbeck" (Ph.D. diss., University of New Mexico, 1973), p. 133.

61. Lionel Trilling, "An American in Spain," *Ernest Hemingway:*

Critiques of Four Major Novels, ed. Carlos Baker (New York: Scribner's, 1962), p. 80.

62. W. M. Frohock, *The Novel of Violence*, p. 189.

63. Mark Schorer, "The Background of a Style," p. 89.

64. Philip Young, *Ernest Hemingway* (New York: Rinehart, 1952), p. 81.

65. Leslie A. Fiedler, *Love and Death*, p. 304.

66. Robert E. Spiller, *The Cycle of American Literature* (New York: New American Library, 1967), p. 206.

67. Sharon Dean, "Lost Ladies," p. 129.

68. Carlos Baker, *Ernest Hemingway: A Life Story*, p. 478.

69. Lillian Ross, "How Do You Like It Now, Gentlemen?" *Hemingway: A Collection of Critical Essays*, ed. Robert P. Weeks (Englewood Cliffs, N.J.: Prentice-Hall, 1962), p. 18.

70. Michael F. Moloney, "Ernest Hemingway: The Missing Third Dimension," *Hemingway and His Critics: An International Anthology*, ed. Carlos Baker (New York: Hill and Wang, 1961), p. 180.

71. Maxwell Geismar, *American Moderns: From Rebellion to Conformity* (New York: Hill and Wang, 1958), p. 59.

72. Ibid., p. 59.

73. Jackson J. Benson, *Hemingway: The Writer's Art of Self-Defense* (Minneapolis: University of Minnesota Press, 1969), p. 51.

74. Frederick J. Hoffman, *The Twenties*, p. 96.

75. *Across the River and into the Trees* was originally published in New York by Scribner's in 1950. All page references apply to the 1950 edition.

76. See André Maurois, "Ernest Hemingway," *Hemingway and His Critics*, ed. Carlos Baker (New York: Hill and Wang, 1961), p. 38.

77. Mimi Reisel Gladstein, "The Indestructible Woman," pp. 96–97.

78. Samuel Shaw, *Ernest Hemingway*, p. 110.

79. Jack Mendelsohn, *Why I Am a Unitarian Universalist* (Boston: Beacon, 1964), pp. 167–68.

80. Eric Berne, *What Do You Say?*, p. 5.

122 NOTES

III. BITCHES AND OTHER SIMPLISTIC ASSUMPTIONS

1. Allen Tate, "Hard-Boiled," *The Merrill Studies in The Sun Also Rises*, ed. William White (Columbus, Ohio: Charles E. Merrill, 1969), p. 18.

2. Edwin Muir, "Fiction [*Fiesta*, by Ernest Hemingway]," *The Merrill Studies in The Sun Also Rises*, ed. William White (Columbus, Ohio: Charles E. Merrill, 1969), p. 15.

3. Theodore Bardacke, "Hemingway's Women," *Ernest Hemingway: The Man and His Work*, ed. John K. M. McCaffery (New York: Avon, 1950), p. 309.

4. Jackson J. Benson, *Hemingway: The Writer's Art of Self-Defense* (Minneapolis: University of Minnesota Press, 1969), p. 30.

5. Mimi Reisel Gladstein, "The Indestructible Woman in the Works of Faulkner, Hemingway, and Steinbeck" (Ph.D. diss., University of New Mexico, 1973), p. 115.

6. Pamella Farley, "Form and Function: The Image of Woman in Selected Works of Hemingway and Fitzgerald" (Ph.D. diss., Pennsylvania State University, 1973), p. 32.

7. See, for example, Aaron Latham, "Unfinished Manuscripts Reveal a Hemingway No One Knew," Chicago *Tribune*, October 17, 1977, Section 3, p. 20.

8. Carlos Baker, *Ernest Hemingway: A Life Story* (New York: Scribner's, 1969), p. 312.

9. *The Sun Also Rises* was originally published in New York by Scribner's in 1926. All page references apply to the 1926 edition.

10. Edmund Wilson, *The Wound and the Bow* (Cambridge: Houghton Mifflin, 1941), p. 238.

11. Philip Young, *Ernest Hemingway* (New York: Rinehart, 1952), p. 56.

12. Joseph Warren Beach, *American Fiction: 1920–1940* (New York: Russell and Russell, 1960), p. 81.

13. Leslie A. Fiedler, *Love and Death in the American Novel* (New York: Criterion, 1960), p. 307.

14. John W. Aldridge, *After the Lost Generation* (New York: McGraw-Hill, 1951), p. 24.

15. James T. Farrell, *"The Sun Also Rises," Ernest Hemingway: Critiques of Four Major Novels*, ed. Carlos Baker (New York: Scribner's, 1962), p. 4.

16. Robert E. Spiller, *The Cycle of American Literature* (New York: New American Library, 1967), p. 207.

17. Roderick Nash, *The Nervous Generation: American Thought, 1917–1930* (Chicago: Rand McNally, 1970), pp. 3–4.

18. Henry Seidel Canby, "A Review of *A Farewell to Arms*," *The Merrill Studies in A Farewell to Arms*, ed. John Graham (Columbus, Ohio: Charles E. Merrill, 1971), p. 14.

19. Ernest Boyd, "Readers and Writers," *The Merrill Studies in The Sun Also Rises*, ed. William White (Columbus, Ohio: Charles E. Merrill, 1969), p. 7.

20. Philip Young, *Ernest Hemingway* (New York: Rinehart, 1952), p. 58.

21. Cleveland B. Chase, "Out of Little, Much," *The Merrill Studies in The Sun Also Rises*, ed. William White (Columbus, Ohio: Charles E. Merrill, 1969), p. 10.

22. T. S. Matthews, "Nothing Ever Happens to the Brave," *The Merrill Studies in A Farewell to Arms*, ed. John Graham (Columbus, Ohio: Charles E. Merrill, 1971), p. 10.

23. Jackson J. Benson, *Hemingway: The Writer's Art*, p. 20.

24. Sheridan Baker, "Jake Barnes and Spring Torrents," *The Merrill Studies in The Sun Also Rises*, ed. William White (Columbus, Ohio: Charles E. Merrill, 1969), p. 47.

25. A. E. Hotchner, *Papa Hemingway* (New York: Random House, 1966), p. 49.

26. Edward M. Brecher, *The Sex Researchers* (Boston: Little, Brown, 1969), pp. 191–94.

27. H.L.P. Resnik and Marvin E. Wolfgang, eds., *Sexual Behaviors: Social, Clinical, and Legal Aspects* (Boston: Little, Brown, 1972), pp. 225–26.

28. Eric Berne, *What Do You Say After You Say Hello? The Psychology of Human Destiny* (New York: Grove, 1972), pp. 31–32.

29. Sheldon Grebstein, "Sex, Hemingway, and the Critics," *The Humanist*, 21 (July-August, 1961), p. 216.

30. See *The Sun Also Rises*, pp. 53, 74, 83, 144, 159.

31. The other stories most frequently described as outstanding by critics are "My Old Man," "The Undefeated," "Hills Like White Elephants," "The Killers," "Fifty Grand," and "The Snows of Kilimanjaro." In the preface to *The Short Stories of Ernest Hemingway*, Hemingway lists his own favorites: "Hills Like White Elephants," "The Short Happy Life of Francis Macomber," "The Snows of Kiliman-

jaro," "In Another Country," "A Way You'll Never Be," "A Clean Well-Lighted Place," and "The Light of the World."

32. Warren Beck, "The Shorter Happy Life of Mrs. Macomber," *Modern Fiction Studies*, 1 (November, 1955), pp. 28–37.

33. Virgil Hutton, "The Short Happy Life of Macomber," *University Review*, 30 (June, 1964), pp. 253–63.

34. Robert B. Holland, "Macomber and the Critics," *Studies in Short Fiction*, 5 (Winter, 1967), pp. 171–78.

35. Ibid., pp. 171–72.

36. Pier Francesco Paolini, "The Hemingway of the Major Works," *Hemingway and His Critics: An International Anthology*, ed. Carlos Baker (New York: Hill and Wang, 1961), p. 137.

37. Oliver Evans, " 'The Snows of Kilimanjaro': A Revaluation," *Hemingway's African Stories: The Stories, Their Sources, Their Critics*, ed. John M. Howell (New York: Scribner's, 1969), p. 155.

38. Naomi Grant, "The Role of Women in the Fiction of Ernest Hemingway" (Ph.D. diss., University of Denver, 1968), pp. 64–65.

39. Lemuel B. Byrd, "Characterization in Ernest Hemingway's Fiction: 1925–1952, with a Dictionary of the Characters" (Ph.D. diss., University of Colorado, 1969), p. 74.

40. Sharon Dean, "Lost Ladies: The Isolated Heroine in the Fiction of Hawthorne, James, Fitzgerald, Hemingway, and Faulkner" (Ph.D. diss., University of New Hampshire, 1973), p. 125.

41. Mimi Reisel Gladstein, "The Indestructible Woman," p. 123.

42. Naomi Grant, "The Role of Women," p. 46.

43. Pier Francesco Paolini, "The Hemingway of the Major Works," p. 137.

44. Warren Beck, "The Shorter Happy Life of Mrs. Macomber," pp. 28–37.

45. The version of "The Short Happy Life of Francis Macomber" used in this study is that found in Ernest Hemingway, *The Short Stories of Ernest Hemingway* (New York: Scribner's, 1938), pp. 3–37. All page references are made to that volume.

46. Edmund Wilson, *The Wound and the Bow*, p. 240.

47. Ray B. West, Jr., "The Unadulterated Sensibility," *Twentieth Century Interpretations of A Farewell to Arms*, ed. Jay Gellens (Englewood Cliffs, N.J.: Prentice-Hall, 1970), p. 25.

48. Pier Francesco Paolini, "The Hemingway of the Major Works," p. 137.

49. John Killinger, *Hemingway and the Dead Gods: A Study in Ex-*

istentialism (Lexington: University of Kentucky Press, 1960), p. 44.

50. Joseph DeFalco, *The Hero in Hemingway's Short Stories* (Pittsburgh: University of Pittsburgh Press, 1963), p. 202.

51. Philip Young, *Ernest Hemingway: A Reconsideration* (University Park: Pennsylvania State University Press, 1966), p. 72.

52. Pamella Farley, "Form and Function," p. 97.

53. Philip Young, *Ernest Hemingway* (New York: Rinehart, 1952), p. 43.

54. Hemingway wrote the 850-page Journal during the years 1954–56. Much of it remains in rough-draft form, though one segment, under the title, "Miss Mary's Lion," was published in three installments in *Sports Illustrated* magazine.

55. Carlos Baker, *Ernest Hemingway: A Life Story*, p. 284.

56. Robert B. Holland, "Macomber and the Critics," p. 171.

57. Edmund Wilson, *The Wound and the Bow*, p. 239.

58. Robert W. Lewis, Jr., *Hemingway on Love* (Austin: University of Texas Press, 1965), p. 103.

59. The version of "The Snows of Kilimanjaro" used for this study is the one found in Ernest Hemingway, *The Short Stories of Ernest Hemingway* (New York: Scribner's, 1938), pp. 52–77. All page references apply to this volume.

60. Carlos Baker, *Hemingway: The Writer as Artist* (Princeton, N.J.: Princeton University Press, 1952), pp. 186–87.

61. Leon Linderoth, *The Female Characters of Ernest Hemingway* (Ph.D. diss., Florida State University, 1966), p. 67.

62. Philip Young, *Ernest Hemingway: A Reconsideration*, p. 74.

63. Leslie A. Fiedler, *Love and Death*, p. 307.

64. Naomi M. Grant, "The Role of Women," p. 34.

65. Oliver Evans, " 'The Snows of Kilimanjaro,' " p. 154.

66. Carlos Baker, *Ernest Hemingway: A Life Story*, p. 322.

67. Edmund Wilson, *The Wound and the Bow*, p. 239.

68. The version of *The Fifth Column* used for this study is that found in the volume, *The Fifth Column and Four Stories of the Spanish Civil War* (New York: Scribner's, 1969), pp. 3–85. All page references apply to that volume.

69. Lionel Trilling, "An American in Spain," *Ernest Hemingway: Critiques of Four Major Novels*, ed. Carlos Baker (Scribner's, 1962), p. 78.

70. Philip Young, *Ernest Hemingway* (New York: Rinehart, 1952), p. 74.

71. Allen Guttmann, " 'Mechanized Doom': Ernest Hemingway and the American View of the Spanish Civil War," *Ernest Hemingway: Critiques of Four Major Novels*, ed. Carlos Baker (New York: Scribner's, 1962), p. 96.

72. Maxwell Geismar, *American Moderns: From Rebellion to Conformity* (New York: Hill and Wang, 1958), p. 58.

73. Carlos Baker, *Ernest Hemingway: A Life Story*, p. 339.

74. Leo Gurko, *The Angry Decade* (New York: Dodd, Mead, 1947), p. 187.

75. John Killinger, *Hemingway and the Dead Gods*, pp. 89–90.

76. Theodore Bardacke, "Hemingway's Women," p. 315.

77. Philip Young, *Ernest Hemingway: A Reconsideration*, p. 103.

78. Lemuel B. Byrd, "Characterization in Ernest Hemingway's Fiction," p. 83.

79. Pamella Farley, "Form and Function," p. 104.

80. Leon Linderoth, "The Female Characters," p. 108.

81. Philip Young, *Ernest Hemingway: A Reconsideration*, p. 102.

82. Carlos Baker, *Hemingway: The Writer as Artist*, p. 235.

83. Robert W. Lewis, Jr., *Hemingway on Love*, p. 145.

84. Alfred Kazin, *On Native Grounds: An Interpretation of Modern American Prose Literature* (Garden City, N.Y.: Doubleday, 1956), p. 262.

IV. THE "MINOR" WOMEN

1. The version of each of the ten stories treated in this chapter is found in Ernest Hemingway, *The Short Stories of Ernest Hemingway* (New York: Scribner's, 1938). All page references apply to that volume.

2. Leon Linderoth, "The Female Characters of Ernest Hemingway" (Ph.D. diss., Florida State University, 1966), p. 106.

3. Naomi M. Grant, "The Role of Women in the Fiction of Ernest Hemingway" (Ph.D. diss., University of Denver, 1968), p. 73.

4. Arthur Waldhorn, *A Reader's Guide to Ernest Hemingway* (New York: Farrar, Straus and Giroux, 1972), p. 44.

5. John W. Aldridge, *After the Lost Generation* (New York: McGraw-Hill, 1951), p. 28.

6. Robert W. Lewis, Jr., *Hemingway on Love* (Austin: University of Texas Press, 1965), p. 9.

7. Jackson J. Benson, *Hemingway: The Writer's Art of Self-Defense* (Minneapolis: University of Minnesota Press, 1969), p. 29.

8. Pamella Farley, "Form and Function: The Image of Woman in Selected Works of Hemingway and Fitzgerald" (Ph.D. diss., Pennsylvania State University, 1973), p. 42.

9. Edward M. Brecher, *The Sex Researchers* (Boston: Little, Brown, 1969), p. 113.

10. Leon Linderoth, "The Female Characters," p. 106.

11. John Killinger, *Hemingway and the Dead Gods: A Study in Existentialism* (Lexington: University of Kentucky Press, 1960), p. 89.

12. Philip Young, *Ernest Hemingway* (New York: Rinehart, 1952), p. 6.

13. Leslie A. Fiedler, *Love and Death in the American Novel* (New York: Criterion, 1960), p. 305.

14. D. H. Lawrence, *"In Our Time:* A Review," *Hemingway: A Collection of Critical Essays*, ed. Robert P. Weeks (Englewood Cliffs, N.J.: Prentice-Hall, 1962), p. 93.

15. Lemuel B. Byrd, "Characterization in Ernest Hemingway's Fiction: 1925–1952, with a Dictionary of the Characters" (Ph.D. diss., University of Colorado, 1969), p. 68.

16. Joseph DeFalco, *The Hero in Hemingway's Short Stories* (Pittsburgh: University of Pittsburgh Press, 1963), p. 41.

17. Ibid., p. 155.

18. Leon Linderoth, "The Female Characters," p. 109.

19. Pamella Farley, "Form and Function," p. 51.

20. Leslie A. Fiedler, *Love and Death*, p. 305.

21. Pamella Farley, "Form and Function," p. 46.

22. Leon Linderoth, "The Female Characters," p. 108.

23. Arthur Waldhorn, *A Reader's Guide to Ernest Hemingway*, p. 107.

24. Theodore Bardacke, "Hemingway's Women," *Ernest Hemingway: The Man and His Work*, ed. John K. M. McCaffery (New York: Avon, 1950), p. 312.

25. H. E. Bates, "Hemingway's Short Stories," *Hemingway and His Critics: An International Anthology*, ed. Carlos Baker (New York: Hill and Wang, 1961), p. 75.

26. D. H. Lawrence, *"In Our Time*: A Review," p. 93.

27. Carlos Baker, *Ernest Hemingway: A Life Story* (New York: Scribner's, 1969), p. 465.

28. Leon Linderoth, "The Female Characters," p. 109.

29. Naomi Grant, "The Role of Women," p. 45.

30. Joseph DeFalco, *The Hero in Hemingway's Short Stories*, p. 36.

31. Carlos Baker, *Hemingway: The Writer as Artist* (Princeton, N.J.: Princeton University Press, 1952), p. 129.

32. Jackson J. Benson, *Hemingway: The Writer's Art of Self-Defense*, p. 18.

33. Philip Young, *Ernest Hemingway* (New York: Rinehart, 1952), p. 81.

34. Carlos Baker, *Ernest Hemingway: A Life Story*, p. 465.

35. Mimi R. Gladstein, "The Indestructible Woman in the Works of Faulkner, Hemingway, and Steinbeck" (Ph.D. diss., University of New Mexico, 1973), p. 101.

36. Jackson J. Benson, *Hemingway: The Writer's Art of Self-Defense*, p. 11.

37. Edmund Wilson, *The Wound and the Bow* (Cambridge: Houghton Mifflin, 1941), p. 238.

38. Theodore Bardacke, "Hemingway's Women," p. 314.

39. John Killinger, *Hemingway and the Dead Gods*, p. 89.

40. Leon Linderoth, "The Female Characters," pp. 105–6.

41. Pamella Farley, "Form and Function," p. 30.

42. Carlos Baker, *Hemingway: The Writer as Artist*, p. 255.

V. HEMINGWAY THE MAN—AND THE WRITER

1. Carlos Baker, *Ernest Hemingway: A Life Story* (New York: Scribner's, 1969), p. 189.

2. Leicester Hemingway, *My Brother, Ernest Hemingway* (New York: World, 1961), p. 52.

3. Carlos Baker, *Ernest Hemingway: A Life Story*, p. 240.

4. Malcolm Cowley, "A Portrait of Mister Papa," *Ernest Hemingway: The Man and His Work*, ed. John K. M. McCaffery (New York: World, 1950), p. 34.

5. Gregory H. Hemingway, *Papa: A Personal Memoir* (Boston: Houghton Mifflin, 1976), p. 53.

6. Carlos Baker, *Ernest Hemingway: A Life Story*, p. 207.

7. Ibid., p. 285.

8. Sheldon N. Grebstein, "The Tough Hemingway and His Hard-Boiled Children," *Tough Guy Writers of the Thirties*, ed. David Mad-

den (Carbondale, Ill.: Southern Illinois University Press, 1968), pp. 23–27.

9. Philip Young, *Ernest Hemingway: A Reconsideration* (University Park: Pennsylvania State University Press, 1966), p. 3.

10. Deming Brown, "Hemingway in Russia," *Hemingway and His Critics: An International Anthology*, ed. Carlos Baker (New York: Hill and Wang, 1961), p. 147.

11. Lincoln Kirstein, "The Canon of Death," *Ernest Hemingway: The Man and His Work*, ed. John K. M. McCaffery (New York: World, 1950), p. 50.

12. Edgar Johnson, "Farewell the Separate Peace," *Ernest Hemingway: The Man and His Work*, ed. John K. M. McCaffery (New York: World, 1950), p. 119.

13. Alfred Kazin, *Bright Book of Life: American Novelists and Storytellers from Hemingway to Mailer* (Boston: Little, Brown, 1971), p. 13.

14. Wyndham Lewis, "The 'Dumb Ox' in Love and War," *Twentieth Century Interpretations of A Farewell to Arms*, ed. Jay Gellens (Englewood Cliffs, N.J.: Prentice-Hall, 1970), p. 73.

15. Mario Praz, "Hemingway in Italy," *Hemingway and His Critics*, ed. Carlos Baker (New York: Hill and Wang, 1961), p. 119.

16. Ivan Kashkeen, "Alive in the Midst of Death: Ernest Hemingway," *Hemingway and His Critics*, ed. Carlos Baker (New York: Hill and Wang, 1961), p. 163.

17. Eric Berne, *What Do You Say After You Say Hello? The Psychology of Human Destiny* (New York: Grove, 1972), pp. 270–71.

18. Philip Young, *Ernest Hemingway* (New York: Rinehart, 1952), pp. 136ff.

19. John W. Aldridge, *After the Lost Generation* (New York: McGraw-Hill, 1951), p. 23.

20. Dwight Macdonald, *Against the American Grain* (New York: Random House, 1962), p. 178.

21. Mark Schorer, "The Background of a Style," *Ernest Hemingway: Critiques of Four Major Novels*, ed. Carlos Baker (New York: Scribner's, 1962), p. 87.

22. Ibid., p. 88.

23. John Killinger, *Hemingway and the Dead Gods: A Study in Existentialism* (Lexington: University of Kentucky Press, 1960), p. 98.

24. Carlos Baker, *Ernest Hemingway: A Life Story*, p. vii.

Bibliography

PRIMARY SOURCES

Hemingway, Ernest. *Across the River and into the Trees*. New York: Scribner's, 1950.

————. *By-Line: Selected Articles and Dispatches of Four Decades*. Edited by William White. New York: Scribner's, 1967.

————. *Death in the Afternoon*. New York: Scribner's, 1932.

————. *A Farewell to Arms*. New York: Scribner's, 1929.

————. *The Fifth Column and Four Stories of the Spanish Civil War*. New York: Scribner's, 1969.

————. *For Whom the Bell Tolls*. New York: Scribner's, 1940.

————. *Green Hills of Africa*. New York: Scribner's, 1935.

————. *Islands in the Stream*. New York: Scribner's, 1970.

————. *A Moveable Feast*. New York: Scribner's, 1964.

————. *The Old Man and the Sea*. New York: Scribner's, 1952.

————. *The Short Stories of Ernest Hemingway*. New York: Scribner's, 1938.

————. *The Sun Also Rises*. New York: Scribner's, 1926.

————. *To Have and Have Not*. New York: Scribner's, 1937.

————. *The Torrents of Spring*. New York: Scribner's, 1926.

SECONDARY SOURCES

Adams, J. Donald. "Ernest Hemingway." *English Journal*, 28 (1939): 87–94.

Aiken, Conrad. "Expatriates." *The Merrill Studies in The Sun Also Rises*. Edited by William White. Columbus, Ohio: Charles E. Merrill, 1969.

Aldridge, John W. *After the Lost Generation: A Critical Study of the Writers of Two Wars*. New York: McGraw-Hill, 1951.

Allen, Hugh. "The Dark Night of Ernest Hemingway." *Catholic World*, 152 (1940): 522–29.

Allen, Michael. "The Unspanish War in *For Whom the Bell Tolls*." *Contemporary Literature*, 13 (Spring, 1972): 204–12.

Anderson, Charles R. "Hemingway's Other Style." *Ernest Hemingway: Critiques of Four Major Novels*. Edited by Carlos Baker. New York: Scribner's, 1962.

Backman, Melvin. "Hemingway: The Matador and the Crucified." *Ernest Hemingway: Critiques of Four Major Novels*. Edited by Carlos Baker. New York: Scribner's, 1962.

Baker, Carlos. "Dangerous Game." *Hemingway's African Stories: The Stories, Their Sources, Their Critics*. Edited by John M. Howell. New York: Scribner's, 1969.

————, ed. *Ernest Hemingway: Critiques of Four Major Novels*. New York: Scribner's, 1962.

————. "Ernest Hemingway: *A Farewell to Arms*," *The Merrill Studies in A Farewell to Arms*. Edited by John Graham. Columbus, Ohio: Charles E. Merrill, 1971.

————. *Ernest Hemingway: A Life Story*. New York: Scribner's, 1969.

————. *Hemingway and His Critics: An International Anthology*. New York: Hill and Wang, 1961.

————. "Hemingway's Ancient Mariner." *Ernest Hemingway: Critiques of Four Major Novels*. Edited by Carlos Baker. New York: Scribner's, 1962.

————. *Hemingway: The Writer as Artist*. Princeton, N.J.: Princeton University Press, 1952.

————. "The Mountain and the Plain." *Ernest Hemingway: Critiques of Four Major Novels*. Edited by Carlos Baker. New York: Scribner's, 1962.

————. "Place, Fact, and Scene in *The Sun Also Rises*," *Ernest Hemingway: Critiques of Four Major Novels*. Edited by Carlos Baker. New York: Scribner's, 1962.

————. "The Spanish Tragedy." *Ernest Hemingway: Critiques of Four Major Novels*. Edited by Carlos Baker. New York: Scribner's, 1962.

Baker, Sheridan. "Jake Barnes and Spring Torrents." *The Merrill Studies in The Sun Also Rises*. Edited by William White. Columbus, Ohio: Charles E. Merrill, 1969.

Bardacke, Theodore. "Hemingway's Women." *Ernest Hemingway: The Man and His Work*. Edited by John K. M. McCaffery. New York: World, 1950.

Barea, Arturo. "Not Spain but Hemingway." *Hemingway and His Critics*. Edited by Carlos Baker. New York: Hill and Wang, 1961.

Barnes, Lois L. "The Helpless Hero of Ernest Hemingway." *Science and Society*, 17 (1953): 1–25.

Bartlett, Phyllis. "Other Countries, Other Wenches." *Modern Fiction Studies*, 3 (Winter, 1957–58): 345–49.

Bater, H. E. "Hemingway's Short Stories." *Hemingway and His Critics*. Edited by Carlos Baker. New York: Hill and Wang, 1961.

Beach, Joseph Warren. *American Fiction 1920–1940*. New York: Russell and Russell, 1960.

———. "How Do You Like It Now, Gentlemen?" *Hemingway and His Critics*. Edited by Carlos Baker. New York: Hill and Wang, 1961.

———. "Style in *For Whom the Bell Tolls*," *Ernest Hemingway: Critiques of Four Major Novels*. Edited by Carlos Baker. New York: Scribner's, 1962.

Beauvoir, Simone de. *The Second Sex*. New York: Knopf, 1952.

Beck, Warren. "The Shorter Happy Life of Mrs. Macomber." *Hemingway's African Stories: The Stories, Their Sources, Their Critics*. Edited by John M. Howell. New York: Scribner's, 1969.

Berne, Eric. *Games People Play*. New York: Grove, 1964.

———. *What Do You Say After You Say Hello? The Psychology of Human Destiny*. New York: Grove, 1972.

Bessie, Alvah C. "Review of *For Whom the Bell Tolls*," *Ernest Hemingway: Critiques of Four Major Novels*. Edited by Carlos Baker. New York: Scribner's, 1962.

Bishop, John Peale. "The Missing All." *Ernest Hemingway: The Man and His Work*. Edited by John K. M. McCaffery. New York: World, 1950.

Boyd, Ernest. "Readers and Writers." *The Merrill Studies in The Sun Also Rises*. Edited by William White. Columbus, Ohio: Charles E. Merrill, 1969.

Boyd, J. D. "Hemingway's 'Soldier's Home.' " *Explicator*, 40 (Fall 1981): 50–51.

Brecher, Edward M. *The Sex Researchers*. Boston: Little, Brown, 1969.

Brown, Deming. "Hemingway in Russia." *Hemingway and His Critics*. Edited by Carlos Baker. New York: Hill and Wang, 1961.

Bruccoli, Matthew J., and C. E. Frazer Clark, Jr. *Fitzgerald/ Hemingway Annual 1975*. Englewood, Colo.: Microcard Editions Books, 1975.

Burgum, Edwin Berry. "Ernest Hemingway and the Psychology of the Lost Generation." *Ernest Hemingway: The Man and His Work*. Edited by John K. M. McCaffery. New York: World, 1950.

Burhans, Clinton S., Jr. "*The Old Man and the Sea*: Hemingway's Tragic Vision of Man." *Ernest Hemingway: Critiques of Four Major Novels*. Edited by Carlos Baker. New York: Scribner's, 1962.

Burnam, Tom. "Primitivism and Masculinity in the Work of Ernest Hemingway." *Modern Fiction Studies*, 1 (August, 1955): 20–24.

Byrd, Lemuel Brian. "Characterization in Ernest Hemingway's Fiction: 1925–52, with a Dictionary of the Characters" (Ph.D. dissertation). University of Colorado, 1969.

Canaday, Nicholas J. "The Motif of the Inner Ring in Hemingway's Fiction." *CEA Critic*, 36 (January 1974): 18–21.

Canby, Henry Seidel. "A Review of *A Farewell to Arms*." *The Merrill Studies in A Farewell to Arms*. Edited by John Graham. Columbus, Ohio: Charles E. Merrill, 1971.

Carpenter, F. I. "Hemingway Achieves the Fifth Dimension." *Ernest Hemingway: A Collection of Criticism*. Edited by Arthur Waldhorn. New York: McGraw-Hill, 1973.

Chase, Cleveland B. "Out of Little, Much." *The Merrill Studies in The Sun Also Rises*. Edited by William White. Columbus, Ohio: Charles E. Merrill, 1969.

Colvert, James B. "Ernest Hemingway's Morality in Action." *American Literature*, 37 (November, 1955): 372–85.

Cousins, Norman. "For Whom the Bells Ring." *Saturday Review of Literature*, 42 (August 22, 1959): 18.

Cowley, Malcolm. "Hemingway at Midnight." *New Republic*, 111 (August 19, 1944): 190–95.

———. "Hemingway and the Hero." *New Republic*, 111 (December 4, 1944): 754–58.

———. "Nightmare and Ritual in Hemingway." *Hemingway: A Col-*

lection of Critical Essays. Edited by Robert P. Weeks. Englewood Cliffs, N.J.: Prentice-Hall, 1962.

———. "A Portrait of Mister Papa." *Ernest Hemingway: The Man and His Work.* Edited by John K. M. McCaffery. New York: World, 1950.

———. "A Review of *A Farewell to Arms.*" *The Merrill Studies in A Farewell to Arms.* Edited by John Graham. Columbus, Ohio: Charles E. Merrill, 1971.

Crane, R. S. "Ernest Hemingway: The Short Happy Life of Francis Macomber." *Hemingway's African Stories: The Stories, Their Sources, Their Critics.* Edited by John M. Howell. New York: Scribner's, 1969.

Crozier, Robert D. "For Thine is the Power and the Glory: Love in *For Whom the Bell Tolls.*" *Papers on Language and Literature,* 10 (Winter, 1974): 76–97.

D'Agostino, Nemi. "The Later Hemingway." *Hemingway: A Collection of Critical Essays.* Edited by Robert P. Weeks. Englewood Cliffs, N.J.: Prentice-Hall, 1962.

Daiches, David. "Ernest Hemingway." *College English,* 2 (May, 1941): 725–36.

Davidson, Arnold E. "The Dantean Perspective in Hemingway's *A Farewell to Arms.*" *Journal of Narrative Technique,* 3 (1973): 121–30.

Dean, Sharon Welch. "Lost Ladies: The Isolated Heroine in the Fiction of Hawthorne, James, Fitzgerald, Hemingway, and Faulkner" (Ph.D. dissertation). University of New Hampshire, 1973.

DeFalco, Joseph. *The Hero in Hemingway's Short Stories.* Pittsburgh: University of Pittsburgh Press, 1963.

Donaldson, S. "Wooing of Ernest Hemingway." *American Literature,* 53 (January 1982): 691–710.

Dussinger, Gloria R. "*The Snows of Kilimanjaro*: Harry's Second Chance." *Hemingway's African Stories: The Stories, Their Sources, Their Critics.* Edited by John M. Howell. New York: Scribner's, 1969.

Eastman, Max. "Bull in the Afternoon." *Ernest Hemingway: The Man and His Work.* Edited by John K. M. McCaffery. New York: World, 1950.

Edel, Leon. "The Art of Evasion." *Hemingway: A Collection of Critical Essays.* Edited by Robert P. Weeks. Englewood Cliffs, N.J.: Prentice-Hall, 1962.

Evans, Oliver. "*The Snows of Kilimanjaro*: A Revaluation." *Heming-*

way's African Stories: The Stories, Their Sources, Their Critics. Edited by John M. Howell. New York: Scribner's, 1969.

Evans, Robert. "Hemingway and the Pale Cast of Thought." Ernest
Hemingway: A Collection of Criticism. Edited by Arthur Waldhorn. New York: McGraw-Hill, 1973.

Fadiman, Clifton. "Ernest Hemingway: An American Byron." Nation, 135 (January 18, 1933): 63–64.

———. "A Review of A Farewell to Arms." The Merrill Studies in
A Farewell to Arms. Edited by John Graham. Columbus, Ohio:
Charles E. Merrill, 1971.

Farley, Pamella. "Form and Function: The Image of Woman in Selected Works of Hemingway and Fitzgerald" (Ph.D. dissertation). Pennsylvania State University, 1973.

Farrell, James T. "The Sun Also Rises." Ernest Hemingway: Critiques of Four Major Novels. Edited by Carlos Baker. New York:
Scribner's, 1962.

Fenimore, Edward. "English and Spanish in For Whom the Bell Tolls."
Ernest Hemingway: The Man and His Work. Edited by John K.
M. McCaffery. New York: World, 1950.

Ferber, Steve. "The Hunts of Papa Hemingway." Argosy, 280 (November 1974): 70–71, 80.

Fiedler, Leslie A. Love and Death in the American Novel. New York:
Criterion, 1960.

Fox, Stephen D. "Hemingway's 'The Doctor and the Doctor's Wife.' "
Arizona Quarterly, 29 (Spring 1973): 19–25.

Friedan, Betty. The Feminine Mystique. New York: Norton, 1963.

Friedman, Norman. "Small Hips, Not War." Twentieth Century
Interpretations of A Farewell to Arms. Edited by Jay Gellens.
Englewood Cliffs, N.J.: Prentice-Hall, 1970.

Friedrich, Otto. "Ernest Hemingway: Joy Through Strength." The
Merrill Studies in A Farewell to Arms. Edited by John Graham. Columbus, Ohio: Charles E. Merrill, 1971.

Frohock, W. M. The Novel of Violence in America. Boston: Beacon,
1964.

Fuchs, Daniel. "Ernest Hemingway, Literary Critic." Ernest Hemingway: A Collection of Criticism. Edited by Arthur Waldhorn. New
York: McGraw-Hill, 1973.

Geismar, Maxwell. American Moderns: From Rebellion to Conformity. New York: Hill and Wang, 1958.

———. Writers in Crisis: The American Novel Between Two Wars.
Boston: Houghton Mifflin, 1942.

Gelfant, Blanche. "Language as a Moral Code." *The Merrill Studies in A Farewell to Arms*. Edited by John Graham. Columbus, Ohio: Charles E. Merrill, 1971.

Gellens, Jay, ed. *Twentieth Century Interpretations of A Farewell to Arms*. Englewood Cliffs, N.J.: Prentice-Hall, 1970.

Georgoudaki, Ekaterini. "Some Comments on 'The Snows of Kilimanjaro.' " *Essays in Literature*, 2 (1973): 49–58.

Gladstein, Mimi Reisel. "The Indestructible Woman in the Works of Faulkner, Hemingway, and Steinbeck" (Ph.D. dissertation). University of New Mexico, 1973.

Goodheart, Eugene. "The Legacy of Ernest Hemingway." *Prairie Schooner*, 30 (Fall, 1956): 212–28.

Gordon, Caroline. "Notes on Hemingway and Kafka." *Sewanee Review*, 57 (1949): 215–26.

Gordon, Caroline and Allen Tate. "The Snows of Kilimanjaro: Commentary." *Hemingway's African Stories: The Stories, Their Sources, Their Critics*. Edited by John M. Howell. New York: Scribner's, 1969.

Graham, John. "Ernest Hemingway: The Meaning of Style." *The Merrill Studies in A Farewell to Arms*. Edited by John Graham. Columbus, Ohio: Charles E. Merrill, 1971.

———, ed. *The Merrill Studies in A Farewell to Arms*. Columbus, Ohio: Charles E. Merrill, 1971.

Grant, Naomi M. "The Role of Women in the Fiction of Ernest Hemingway" (Ph.D. dissertation). University of Denver, 1968.

Gray, James. "Tenderly Tolls the Bell." *Ernest Hemingway: The Man and His Work*. Edited by John K. M. McCaffery. New York: World, 1950.

Grebstein, Sheldon Norman. "Sex, Hemingway, and the Critics." *The Humanist*, 21 (July-August 1961): 212–18.

———. "The Tough Hemingway and His Hard-Boiled Children." *Tough Guy Writers of the Thirties*. Edited by David Madden. Carbondale, Ill.: Southern Illinois University Press, 1968.

Greer, Germaine. *The Female Eunuch*. New York: Bantam, 1972.

Gurko, Leo. *The Angry Decade*. New York: Dodd, Mead, 1947.

Guttmann, Allen. " 'Mechanized Doom': Ernest Hemingway and the American View of the Spanish Civil War." *Ernest Hemingway: Critiques of Four Major Novels*. Edited by Carlos Baker. New York: Scribner's, 1962.

Halliday, E. M. "Hemingway's Ambiguity: Symbolism and Irony."

Ernest Hemingway: Critiques of Four Major Novels. Edited by Carlos Baker. New York: Scribner's, 1962.

———. "Hemingway's Narrative Perspective." *Ernest Hemingway: Critiques of Four Major Novels*. Edited by Carlos Baker. New York: Scribner's, 1962.

Hamalian, Leo. "Hemingway as Hunger Artist." *Literary Review*, 16 (Fall 1972): 5–13.

Hanneman, Andre. *Ernest Hemingway: A Comprehensive Bibliography*. Princeton, N.J.: Princeton University Press, 1967.

Harada, Keiichi. "The Marlin and the Shark: A Note on *The Old Man and the Sea*." *Hemingway and His Critics*. Edited by Carlos Baker. New York: Hill and Wang, 1961.

Heiney, Donald. *Recent American Literature*. Woodbury, N.Y.: Barron's Educational Series, 1958.

Hemingway, Ernest. "The Original Conclusion to *A Farewell to Arms*." *Ernest Hemingway: Critiques of Four Major Novels*. Edited by Carlos Baker. New York: Scribner's, 1962.

Hemingway, Gregory H. *Papa: A Personal Memoir*. Boston: Houghton Mifflin, 1976.

Hemingway, Leicester. *My Brother, Ernest Hemingway*. Cleveland and New York: World, 1961.

Hemingway, Mary Welsh. *How It Was*. New York: Knopf, 1976.

Hemphill, George. "Hemingway and James." *Ernest Hemingway: The Man and His Work*. Edited by John K. M. McCaffery. New York: World, 1950.

Hoffman, Frederick J. *The 20's: American Writing in the Postwar Decade*. New York: Macmillan, 1949.

———. "The Secret Wound." *Twentieth Century Interpretations of A Farewell to Arms*. Edited by Jay Gellens. Englewood Cliffs, N.J.: Prentice-Hall, 1970.

Holland, Robert B. "Macomber and the Critics." *Hemingway's African Stories: The Stories, Their Sources, Their Critics*. Edited by John M. Howell. New York: Scribner's, 1969.

Hotchner, A. E. *Papa Hemingway: A Personal Memoir*. New York: Random House, 1966.

Howell, John M., ed. *Hemingway's African Stories: The Stories, Their Sources, Their Critics*. New York: Scribner's, 1969.

Janeway, Elizabeth. *Man's World, Woman's Place*. New York: Morrow, 1975.

Johnson, Edgar. "Farewell the Separate Peace." *Ernest Hemingway:*

BIBLIOGRAPHY **139**

The Man and His Work. Edited by John K. M. McCaffery. New York: World, 1950.

Johnson, James. "The Adolescent Hero: A Trend in Modern Fiction." *Twentieth Century Literature*, 5 (April, 1959): 3–11.

Johnston, K. G. "Nick/Mike Adams? The Hero's Name in 'Cross-Country Snow.' " *American Notes and Queries*, 20 (September/October 1981): 16–18.

Kashkeen, Ivan. "Alive in the Midst of Death: Ernest Hemingway." *Hemingway and His Critics.* Edited by Carlos Baker. New York: Hill and Wang, 1961.

Kashkeen, J. "Ernest Hemingway: A Tragedy of Craftsmanship." *Ernest Hemingway: The Man and His Work.* Edited by John K. M. McCaffery. New York: World, 1950.

Kazin, Alfred. *Bright Book of Life: American Novelists and Storytellers from Hemingway to Mailer.* Boston: Little, Brown, 1971.

———. *On Native Grounds: An Interpretation of Modern American Prose Literature.* Garden City, N.Y.: Doubleday, 1956.

Kenney, William. "Hunger and the American Dream in *To Have and Have Not.*" *CEA Critic*, 36 (January 1974): 26–28.

Killinger, John. *Hemingway and the Dead Gods: A Study in Existentialism.* Lexington: University of Kentucky Press, 1960.

Kirstein, Lincoln. "The Canon of Death." *Ernest Hemingway: The Man and His Work.* Edited by John K. M. McCaffery. New York: World, 1950.

Klimo, Vernon (Jake) and Will Oursler. *Hemingway and Jake: An Extraordinary Friendship.* Garden City, N.Y.: Doubleday, 1972.

Kobler, J.F. "Let's Run Catherine Barkley Up the Flagpole and See Who Salutes." *CEA Critic*, 36 (January 1974): 4–10.

Lawrence, D. H. "*In Our Time*: A Review." *Hemingway: A Collection of Critical Essays.* Edited by Robert P. Weeks. Englewood Cliffs, N.J.: Prentice-Hall, 1962.

Levin, Harry. "Observations on the Style of Ernest Hemingway." *Hemingway: A Collection of Critical Essays.* Edited by Robert P. Weeks. Englewood Cliffs, N.J.: Prentice-Hall, 1962.

Lewis, Robert W., Jr. "Hemingway in Italy: Making It Up." *Journal of Modern Literature*, 9 (May 1982): 209–36.

———. *Hemingway on Love.* Austin: University of Texas Press, 1965.

———. "The Tough Romance." *Twentieth Century Interpretations of A Farewell to Arms.* Edited by Jay Gellens. Englewood Cliffs, N.J.: Prentice-Hall, 1970.

Lewis, Wyndham. "The 'Dumb Ox' in Love and War." *Twentieth Century Interpretations of A Farewell to Arms*. Edited by Jay Gellens. Englewood Cliffs, N.J.: Prentice-Hall, 1970.

Light, James F. "The Religion of Death in *A Farewell to Arms*." *Ernest Hemingway: Critiques of Four Major Novels*. Edited by Carlos Baker. New York: Scribner's, 1962.

Linderoth, Leon Walter. "The Female Characters of Ernest Hemingway" (Ph.D. dissertation). Florida State University, 1966.

Lynn, S. K. "Hemingway's Private War." *Commentary*, 72 (July 1981): 24–33.

Macdonald, Dwight. *Against the American Grain*. New York: Random House, 1952.

MacDonald, Scott. "Hemingway's 'The Snows of Kilimanjaro': Three Critical Problems." *Studies in Short Fiction*, 11 (Winter 1974): 67–74.

Madden, David, ed. *Tough Guy Writers of the Thirties*. Carbondale, Ill.: Southern Illinois University Press, 1968.

Matthews, T. S. "Nothing Ever Happens to the Brave." *The Merrill Studies in A Farewell to Arms*. Edited by John Graham. Columbus, Ohio: Charles E. Merrill, 1971.

Maurois, André. "Ernest Hemingway." *Hemingway and His Critics*. Edited by Carlos Baker. New York: Hill and Wang, 1961.

McCaffery, John K. M., ed. *Ernest Hemingway: The Man and His Work*. New York: World, 1950.

McSweeney, Kerry. "The First Hemingway Hero." *Dalhousie Review*, 52 (Summer 1972): 308–14.

Mendelsohn, Jack. *Why I Am a Unitarian Universalist*. Boston: Beacon, 1964.

Millett, Kate. *Sexual Politics*. New York: Avon, 1971.

Moloney, Michael F. "Ernest Hemingway: The Missing Third Dimension." *Hemingway and His Critics*. Edited by Carlos Baker. New York: Hill and Wang, 1961.

Montgomery, Marion. "The Leopard and the Hyena: Symbol and Meaning in *The Snows of Kilimanjaro*." *Hemingway's African Stories: The Stories, Their Sources, Their Critics*. Edited by John M. Howell. New York: Scribner's, 1969.

Moody, Raymond, Jr. *Life After Life*. New York: Bantam, 1975.

———. *Reflections on Life After Life*. New York: Bantam, 1977.

Morris, Lawrence S. "Warfare in Man and Among Men." *The Merrill Studies in The Sun Also Rises*. Edited by William White. Columbus, Ohio: Charles E. Merrill, 1969.

Muir, Edwin. "Fiction [*Fiesta*, by Ernest Hemingway]." *The Merrill Studies in The Sun Also Rises*. Edited by William White. Columbus, Ohio: Charles E. Merrill, 1969.

Muller, Herbert J. *Modern Fiction: A Study in Values*. New York: Funk and Wagnalls, 1937.

Nagel, James. "The Narrative Method of 'The Short Happy Life of Francis Macomber.' " *Research Studies*, 41 (1973): 18–27.

Nash, Roderick. *The Nervous Generation: American Thought, 1917–1930*. Chicago: Rand McNally, 1970.

O'Faolain, Sean. "A Clean, Well-Lighted Place." *Hemingway: A Collection of Critical Essays*. Edited by Robert P. Weeks. Englewood Cliffs, N.J.: Prentice-Hall, 1962.

Oldsey, Bernard S. "Hemingway's Old Men." *Modern Fiction Studies*, 1 (August 1955): 32–35.

———. "The Snows of Ernest Hemingway." *Ernest Hemingway: A Collection of Criticism*. Edited by Arthur Waldhorn. New York: McGraw-Hill, 1973.

Oppel, Horst. "Hemingway's *Across the River and Into the Trees*." *Hemingway and His Critics*. Edited by Carlos Baker. New York: Hill and Wang, 1961.

Paolini, Pier Francesco. "The Hemingway of the Major Works." *Hemingway and His Critics*. Edited by Carlos Baker. New York: Hill and Wang, 1961.

Paul, Elliot. "Hemingway and the Critics." *Ernest Hemingway: The Man and His Work*. Edited by John K. M. McCaffery. New York: World, 1950.

Petry, A. H. "Hemingway's 'The Light of the World.' " *Explicator*, 40 (Spring 1982): 46.

Phillips, William. "Male-ism and Morality." *American Mercury*, 75 (October 1952): 93–98.

Pierce, J. F. "The Car as Symbol in Hemingway's 'The Short Happy Life of Francis Macomber.' " *The South Central Bulletin*, 32 (Winter 1972), 230–32.

Plimpton, George. "An Interview with Ernest Hemingway." *Hemingway and His Critics*. Edited by Carlos Baker. New York: Hill and Wang, 1961.

Praz, Mario. "Hemingway in Italy." *Hemingway and His Critics*. Edited by Carlos Baker. New York: Hill and Wang, 1961.

Reid, Stephen A. "The Oedipal Pattern in Hemingway's 'The Capitol of the World.' " *Literature and Psychology*, 13 (Spring 1963): 37–43.

Resnik, H.L.P. and Marvin E. Wolfgang, editors. *Sexual Behaviors: Social, Clinical, and Legal Aspects*. Boston: Little, Brown, 1972.

Robinson, Charles E. "James T. Farrell's Critical Estimate of Hemingway." *Fitzgerald/Hemingway Annual 1973*, pp. 209–14.

Robinson, Forrest D. "Frederick Henry: The Hemingway Hero as Storyteller." *CEA Critic*, 34 (Fall 1972): 13–16.

Ross, Lillian. "How Do You Like It Now, Gentlemen?" *Hemingway: A Collection of Critical Essays*. Edited by Robert P. Weeks. Englewood Cliffs, N.J.: Prentice-Hall, 1962.

Rovit, Earl. "Learning to Care." *Twentieth Century Interpretations of A Farewell to Arms*. Edited by Jay Gellens. Englewood Cliffs, N.J.: Prentice-Hall, 1970.

———. "*The Sun Also Rises*: An Essay in Applied Principles." *The Merrill Studies in The Sun Also Rises*. Edited by William White. Columbus, Ohio: Charles E. Merrill, 1969.

Savage, D.S. "Ciphers at the Front." *Twentieth Century Interpretations of A Farewell to Arms*. Edited by Jay Gellens. Englewood Cliffs, N.J.: Prentice-Hall, 1970.

Schneider, Daniel J. "Hemingway's *A Farewell to Arms*: The Novel as Pure Poetry." *The Merrill Studies in A Farewell to Arms*. Edited by John Graham. Columbus, Ohio: Charles E. Merrill, 1971.

Schorer, Mark. "The Background of a Style." *Ernest Hemingway: Critiques of Four Major Novels*. Edited by Carlos Baker. New York: Scribner's, 1962.

———. "With Grace Under Pressure." *Ernest Hemingway: Critiques of Four Major Novels*. Edited by Carlos Baker. New York: Scribner's, 1962.

Schwartz, Delmore. "Ernest Hemingway's Literary Situation." *Ernest Hemingway: The Man and His Work*. Edited by John K. M. McCaffery. New York: World, 1950.

Shaw, Samuel. *Ernest Hemingway*. New York: Frederick Ungar, 1973.

Shelton, Frank W. "The Family in Hemingway's Nick Adams Stories." *Studies in Short Fiction*, 2 (Summer 1974): 303–5.

Spilka, Mark. "The Death of Love in *The Sun Also Rises*." *Ernest Hemingway: Critiques of Four Major Novels*. Edited by Carlos Baker. New York: Scribner's, 1962.

Spiller, Robert E. *The Cycle of American Literature: An Essay in Historical Criticism*. New York: New American Library, 1955.

Spivey, Ted R. "Hemingway's Pursuit of Happiness on the Open

Road." *Emory University Quarterly*, 11 (December 1955): 240–52.

Stein, Gertrude. "Hemingway in Paris." *Ernest Hemingway: The Man and His Work*. Edited by John K. M. McCaffery. New York: World, 1950.

Tate, Allen. "Hard-Boiled." *The Merrill Studies in The Sun Also Rises*. Edited by William White. Columbus, Ohio: Charles E. Merrill, 1969.

Todd, B. E. "A Review of *A Farewell to Arms*." *The Merrill Studies in A Farewell to Arms*. Edited by John Graham. Columbus, Ohio: Charles E. Merrill, 1971.

Trilling, Lionel. "An American in Spain." *Ernest Hemingway: Critiques of Four Major Novels*. Edited by Carlos Baker. New York: Scribner's, 1962.

Vandersee, Charles. "The Stopped Worlds of Frederick Henry." *The Merrill Studies in A Farewell to Arms*. Edited by John Graham. Columbus, Ohio: Charles E. Merrill, 1971.

Waggoner, Hyatt H. "Ernest Hemingway." *Christian Scholar*, 38 (June 1955): 114–20.

Waldhorn, Arthur. "Artist and Adventurer: A Biographical Sketch." *Ernest Hemingway: A Collection of Criticism*. Edited by Arthur Waldhorn. New York: McGraw-Hill, 1973.

————, ed. *Ernest Hemingway: A Collection of Criticism*. New York: McGraw-Hill, 1973.

————. *A Reader's Guide to Ernest Hemingway*. New York: Farrar, Straus and Giroux, 1972.

Waldmeir, Joseph. "*Confiteor Hominen*: Ernest Hemingway's Religion of Man" *Ernest Hemingway: Critiques of Four Major Novels*. Edited by Carlos Baker. New York: Scribner's, 1962.

Weeks, Robert P., ed. *Hemingway: A Collection of Critical Essays*. Englewood Cliffs, N.J.: Prentice–Hall, 1962.

————. "Hemingway and the Spectatorial Attitude." *Western Humanities Review*, 11 (Summer 1957): 277–81.

West, Ray B., Jr. "The Biological Trap." *Hemingway: A Collection of Critical Essays*. Edited by Robert P. Weeks. Englewood Cliffs, N.J.: Prentice-Hall, 1962.

————. "*A Farewell to Arms*." *Ernest Hemingway: Critiques of Four Major Novels*. Edited by Carlos Baker. New York: Scribner's, 1962.

————. "The Unadulterated Sensibility." *Twentieth Century Inter-*

pretations of A Farewell to Arms. Edited by Jay Gellens. Englewood Cliffs, N.J.: Prentice-Hall, 1970.

Wexler, J. "ERA for Hemingway: A Feminine Defense of *A Farewell to Arms*." *Georgia Review*, 35 (Spring 1981): 111–23.

White, William, ed. *The Merrill Studies in The Sun Also Rises*. Columbus, Ohio: Charles E. Merrill, 1969.

Widmayer, J. A. "Hemingway's Hemingway Parodies." *Studies in Short Fiction*, 18 (Fall 1981): 433–38.

Wilson, Douglas. "Ernest Hemingway, The Nick Adams Stories." *Western Humanities Review*, 27 (1973): 295–99.

Wilson, Edmund. "Emergence of Ernest Hemingway." *Hemingway and His Critics*. Edited by Carlos Baker. New York: Hill and Wang, 1961.

———. *The Wound and the Bow: Seven Studies in Literature*. Boston: Houghton Mifflin, 1941.

Winston, Alexander. "If He Hadn't Been a Genius He Would Have Been a Cad." *American Society Legion of Honor Magazine*, 43 (1972): 25–40.

Wyatt, D. M. "Hand of the Master." *Virginia Quarterly Review*, 56 (Spring 1980): 312–19.

Young, Philip. "A Defense." *Hemingway: A Collection of Critical Essays*. Edited by Robert P. Weeks. Englewood Cliffs, N.J.: Prentice-Hall, 1962.

———. *Ernest Hemingway*. New York: Rinehart, 1952.

———. *Ernest Hemingway* (pamphlet). Minneapolis: University of Minnesota Press, 1959.

———. *Ernest Hemingway: A Reconsideration*. University Park: Pennsylvania State University Press, 1966.

———. "Loser Take Nothing." *Twentieth Century Interpretations of A Farewell to Arms*. Edited by Jay Gellens. Englewood Cliffs, N.J.: Prentice-Hall, 1970.

———. "*The Sun Also Rises*: A Commentary." *Ernest Hemingway: Critiques of Four Major Novels*. Edited by Carlos Baker. New York: Scribner's, 1962.

Index

ABOUT THE AUTHOR

ROGER WHITLOW is Professor of English at Eastern Illinois University. He is the author of three other books, *Black American Literature, The Darker Vision,* and *Many Yankee Faces,* and numerous articles on American literature.